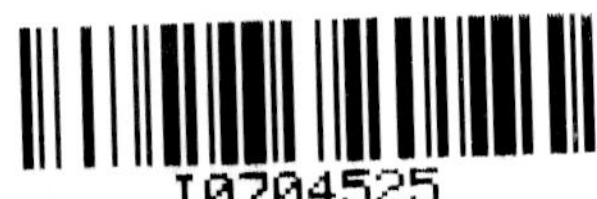

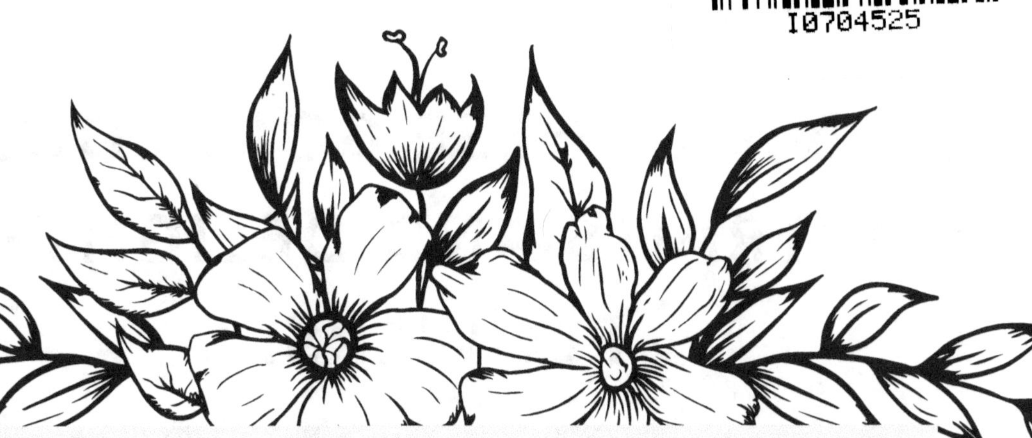

Fabulous Faces
AND FLOWERS

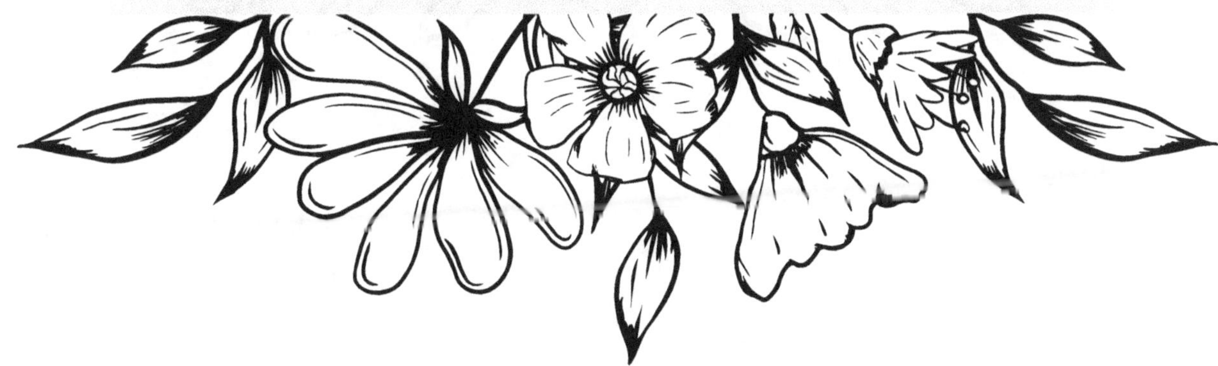

ENJOY THESE GORGEOUS PORTRAITS AND DELIGHTFUL FLOWERS.

RELAX AND COLOR!

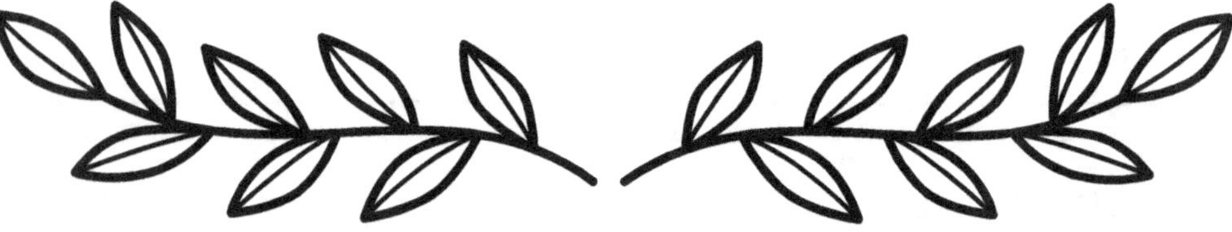

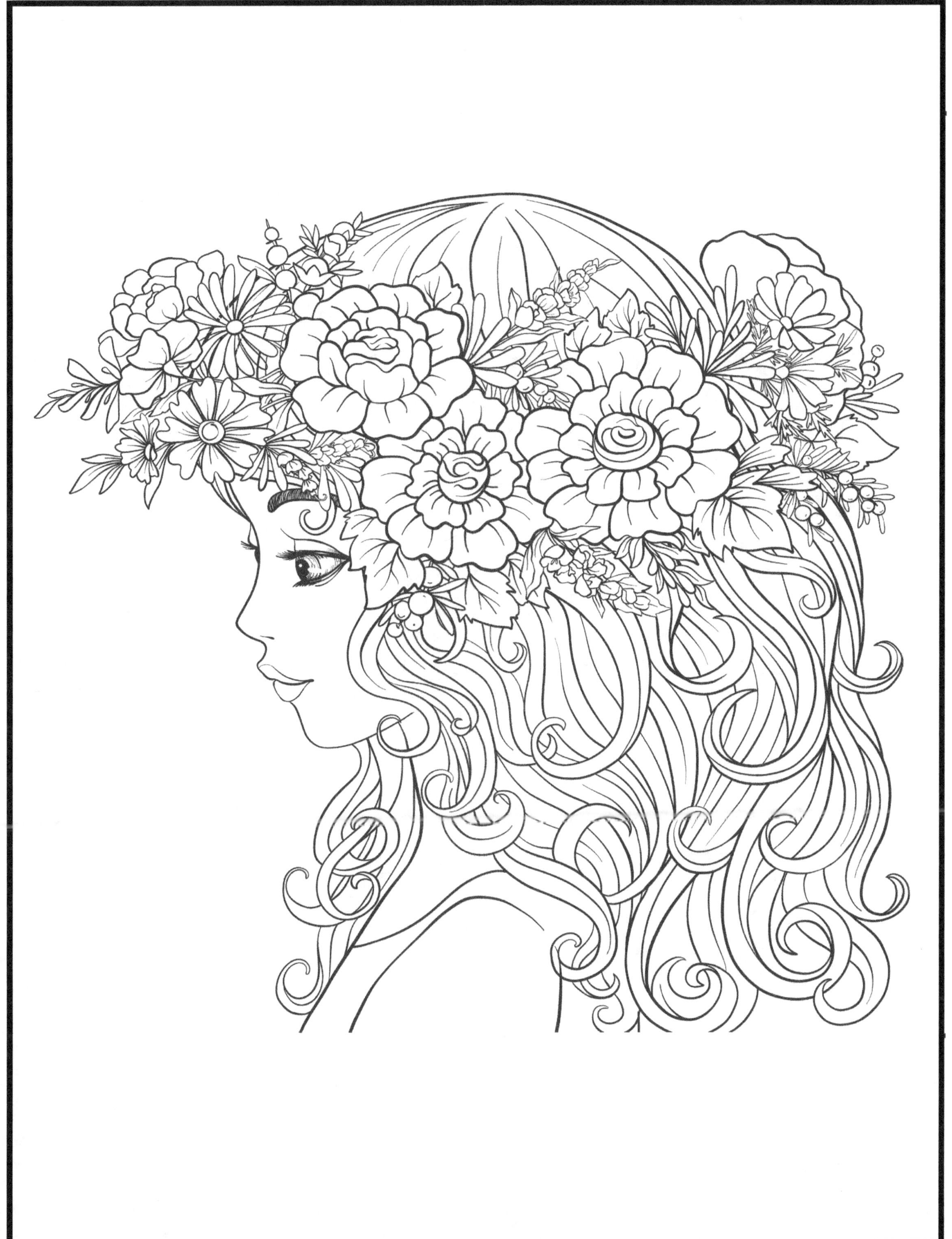

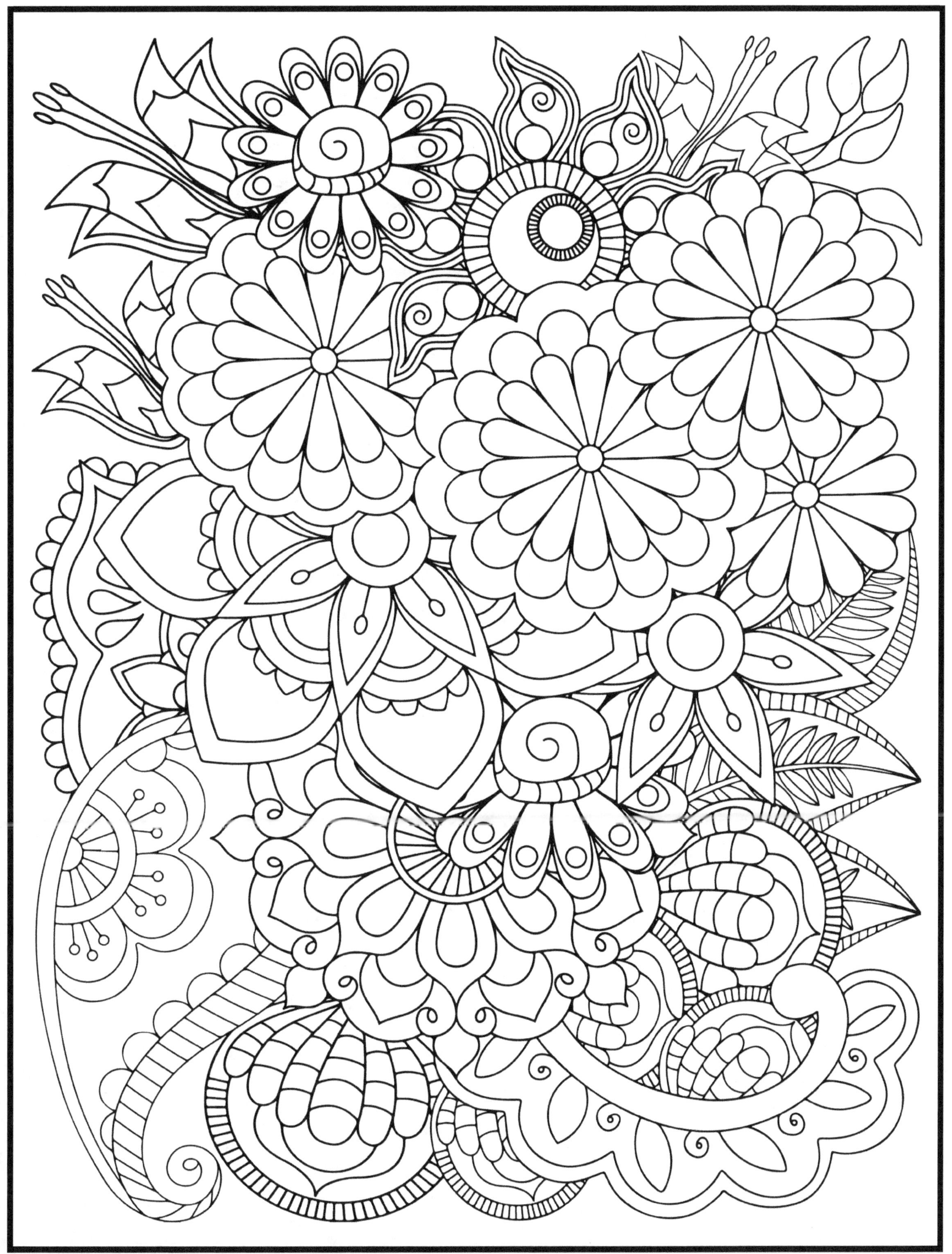

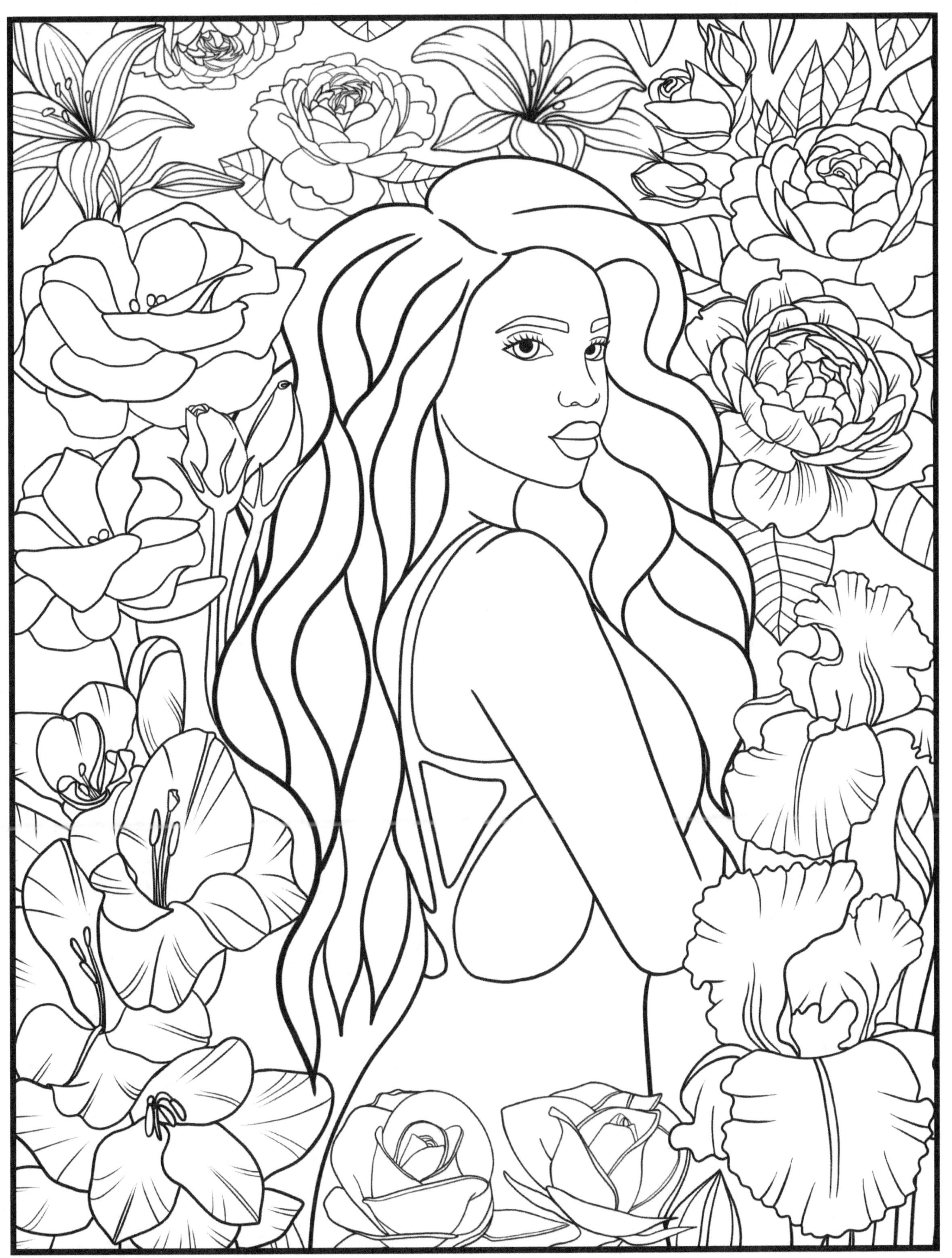

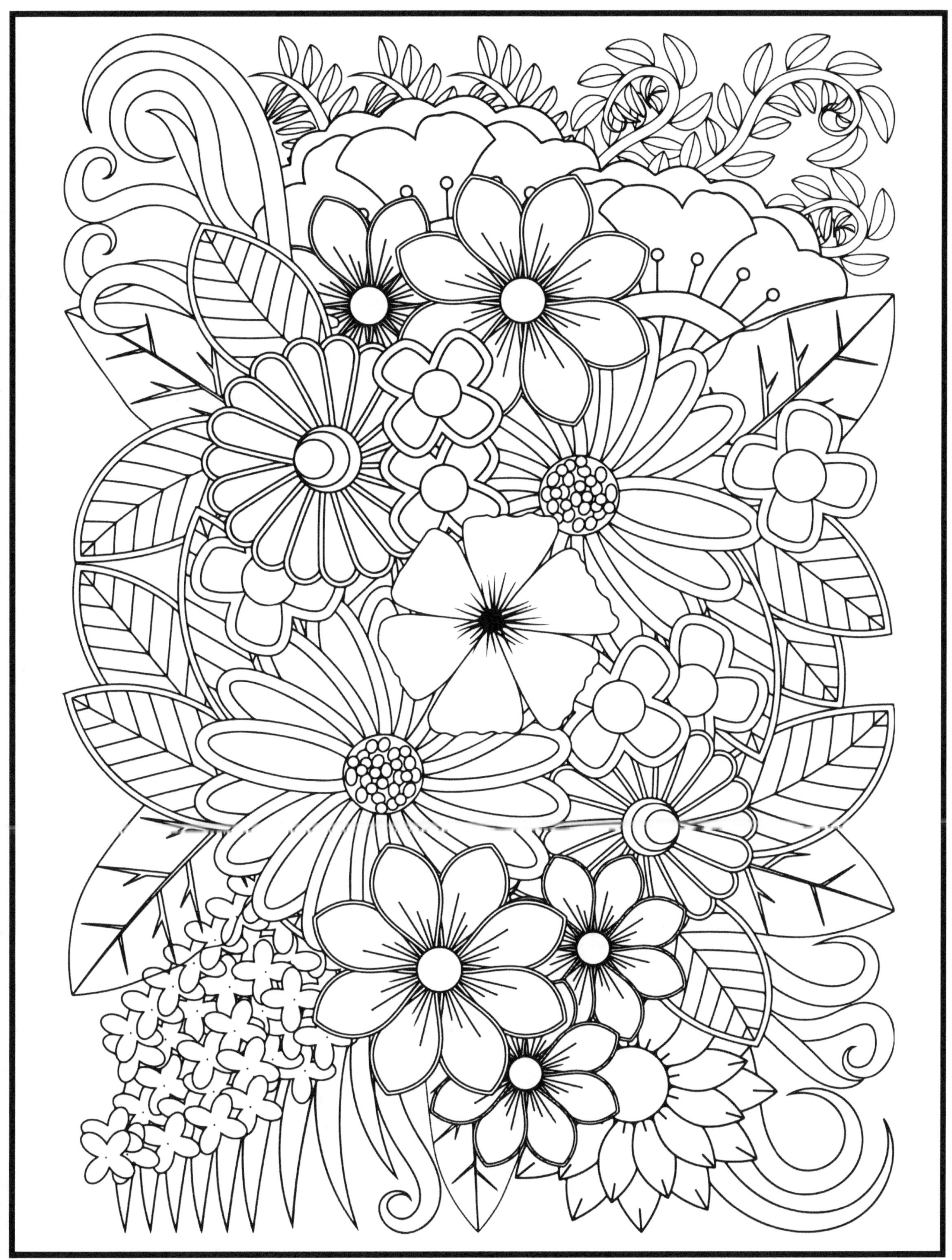

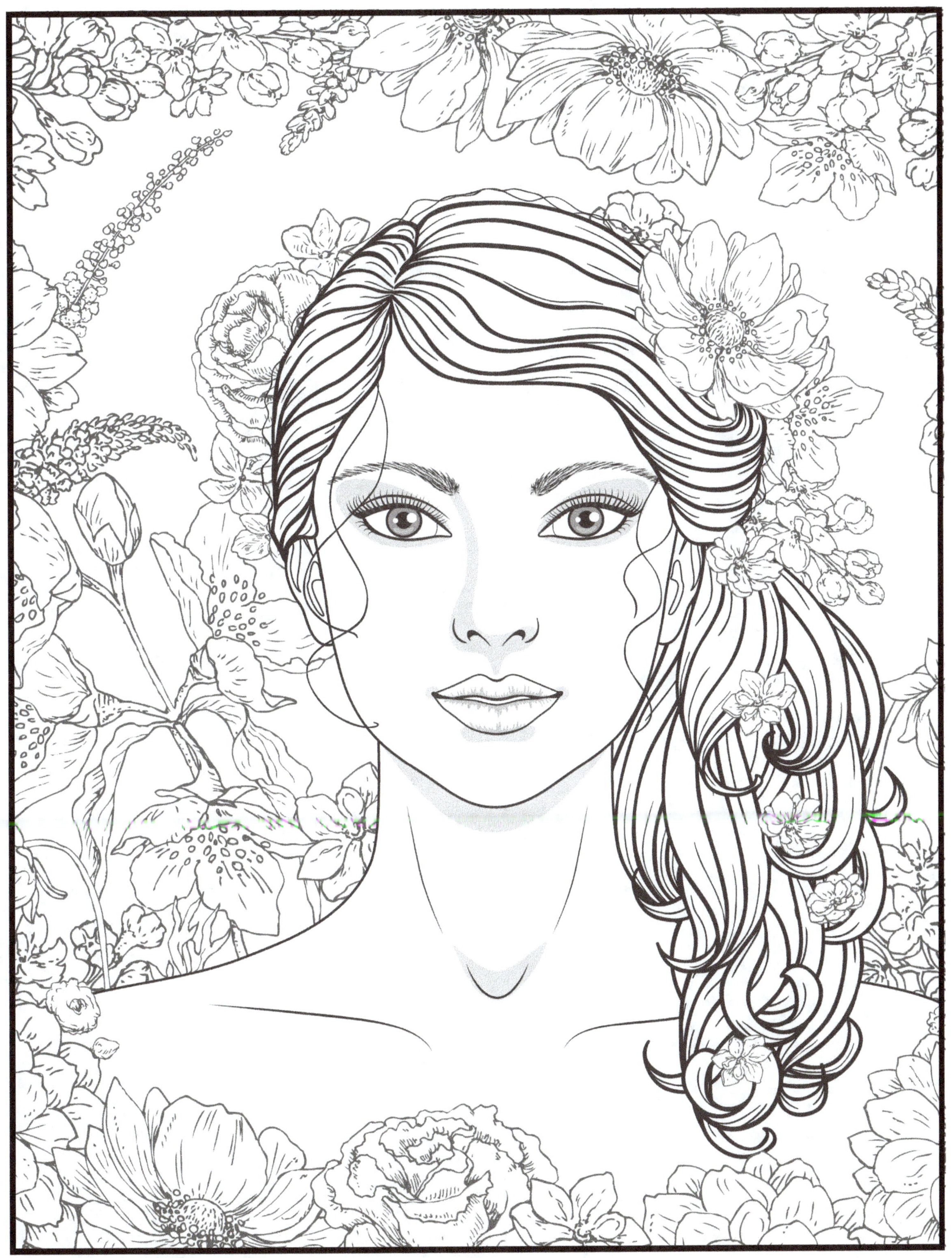

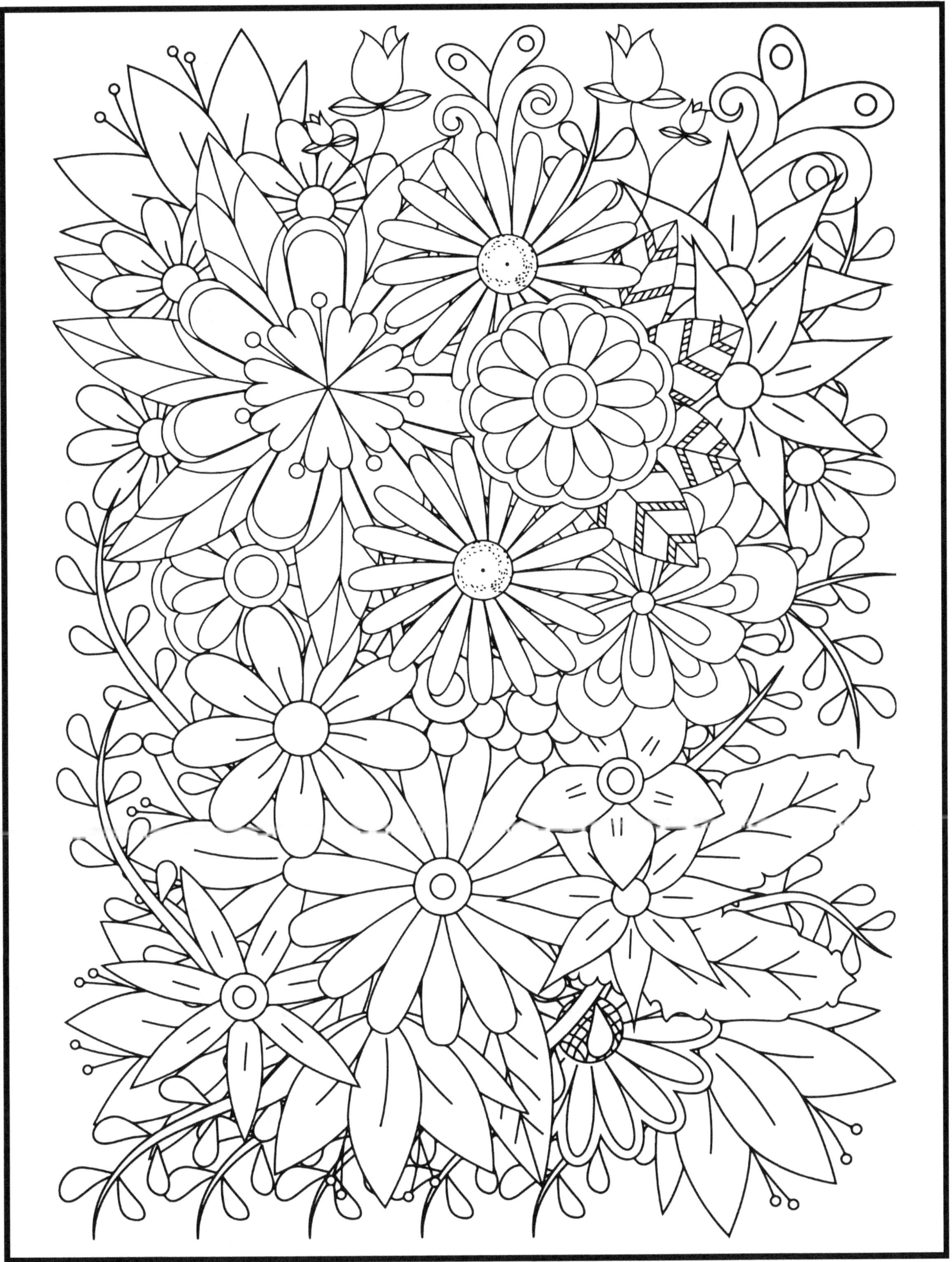

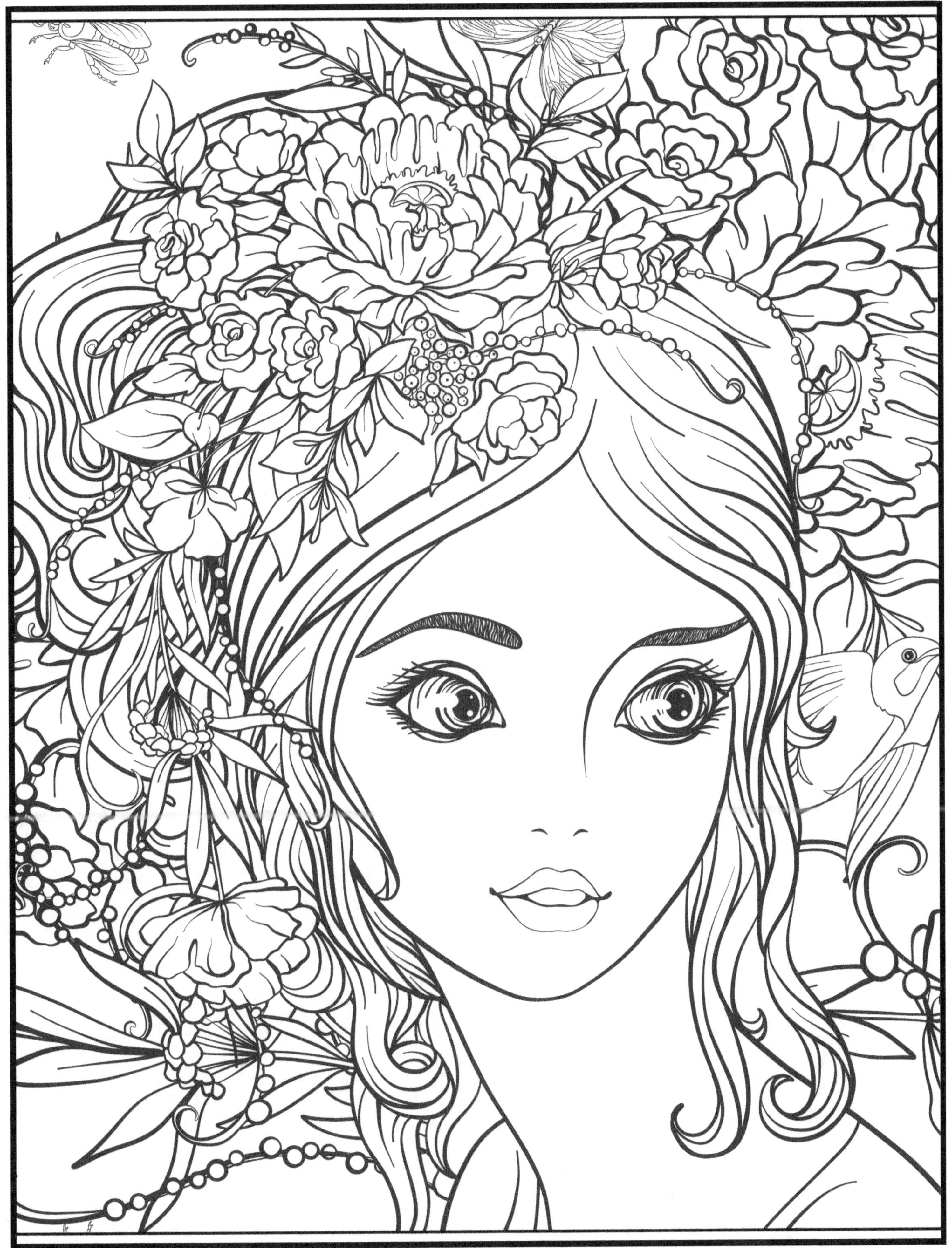

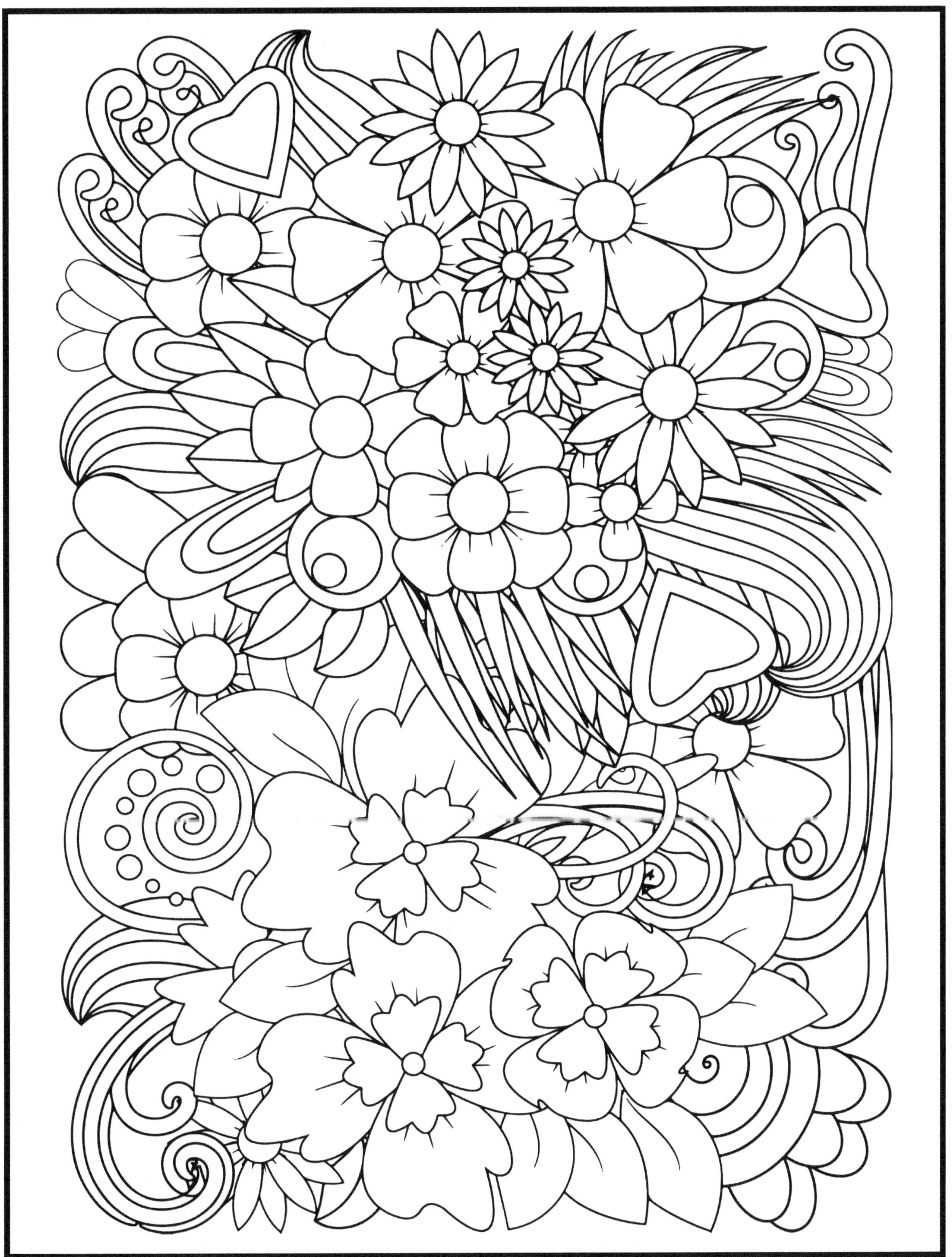

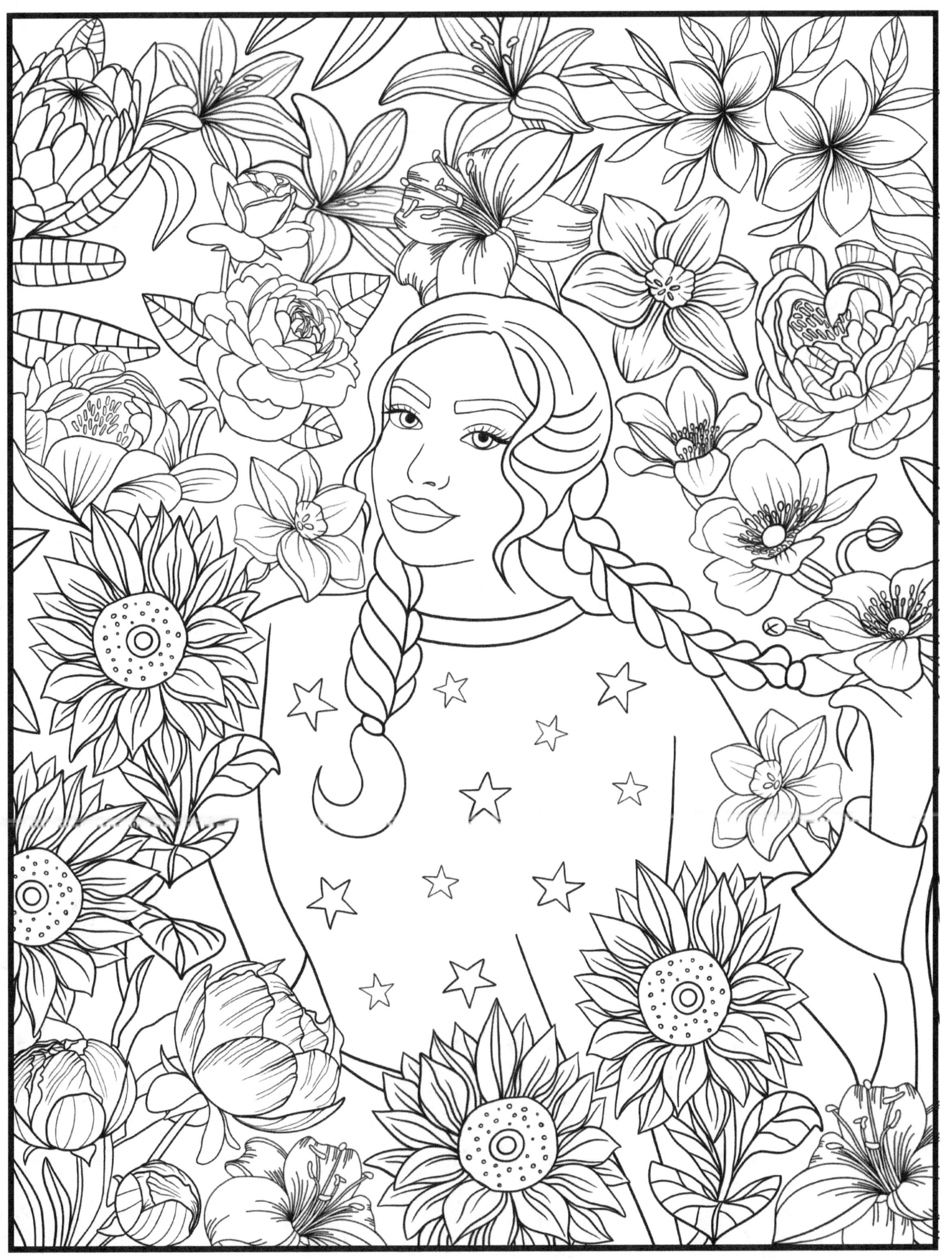

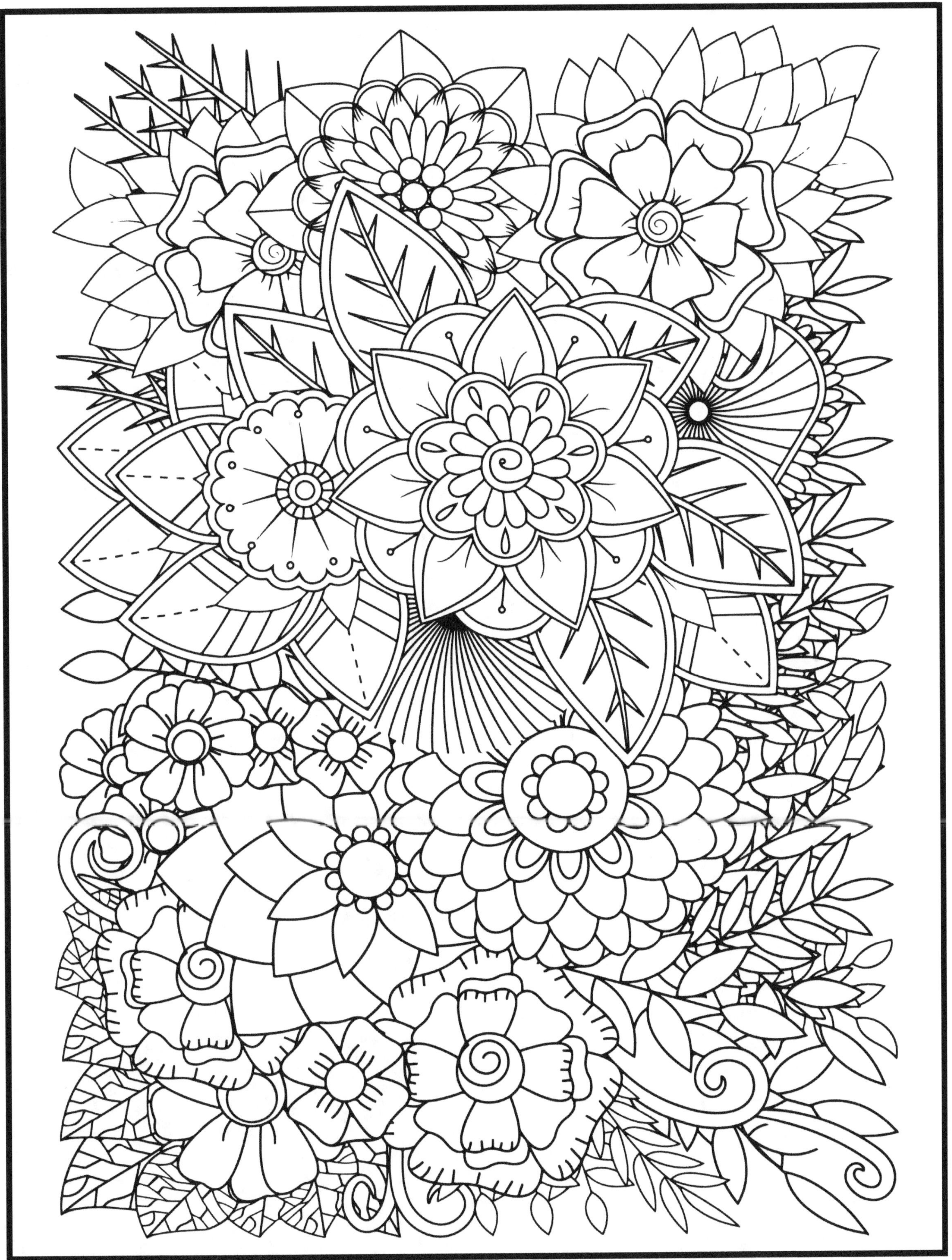

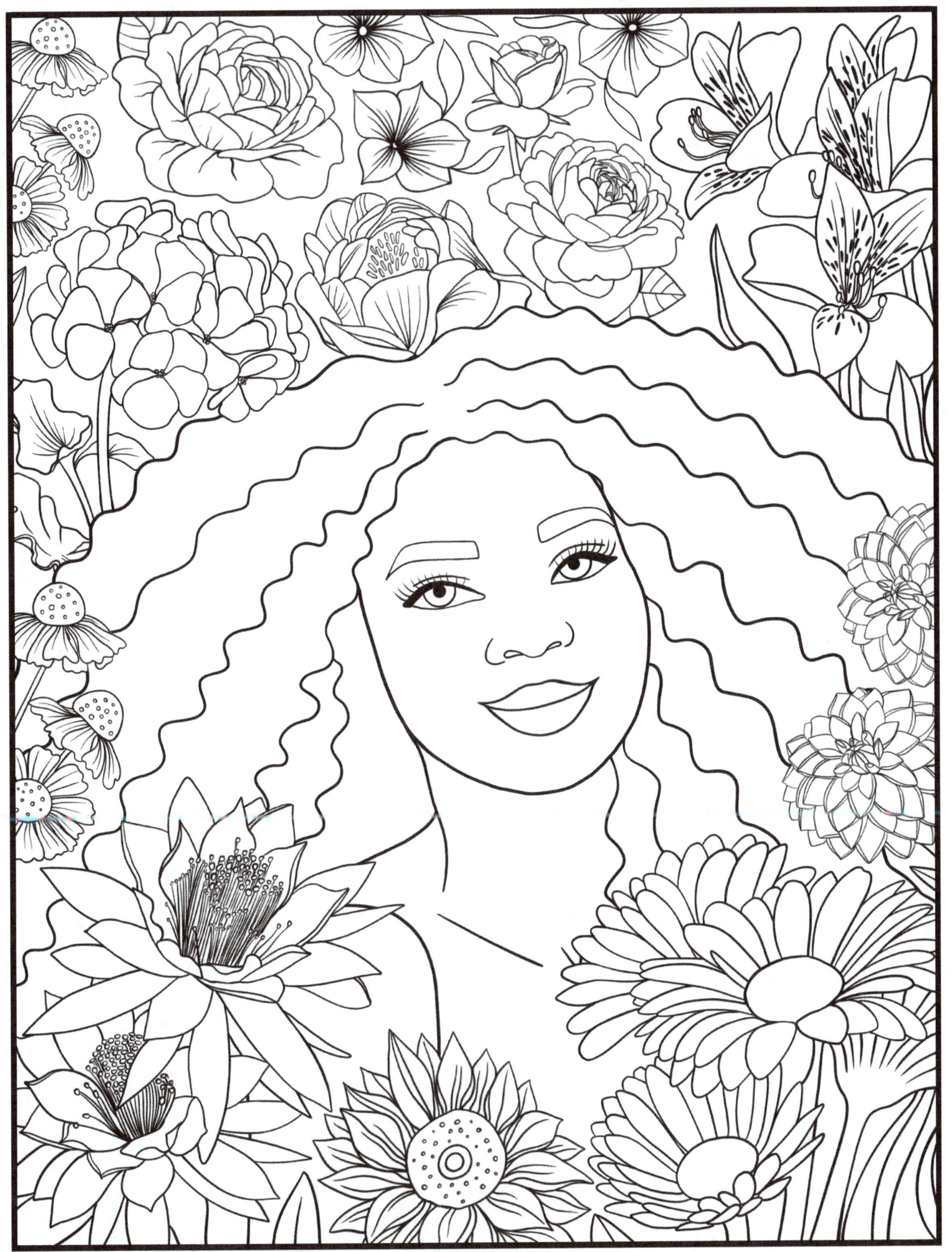

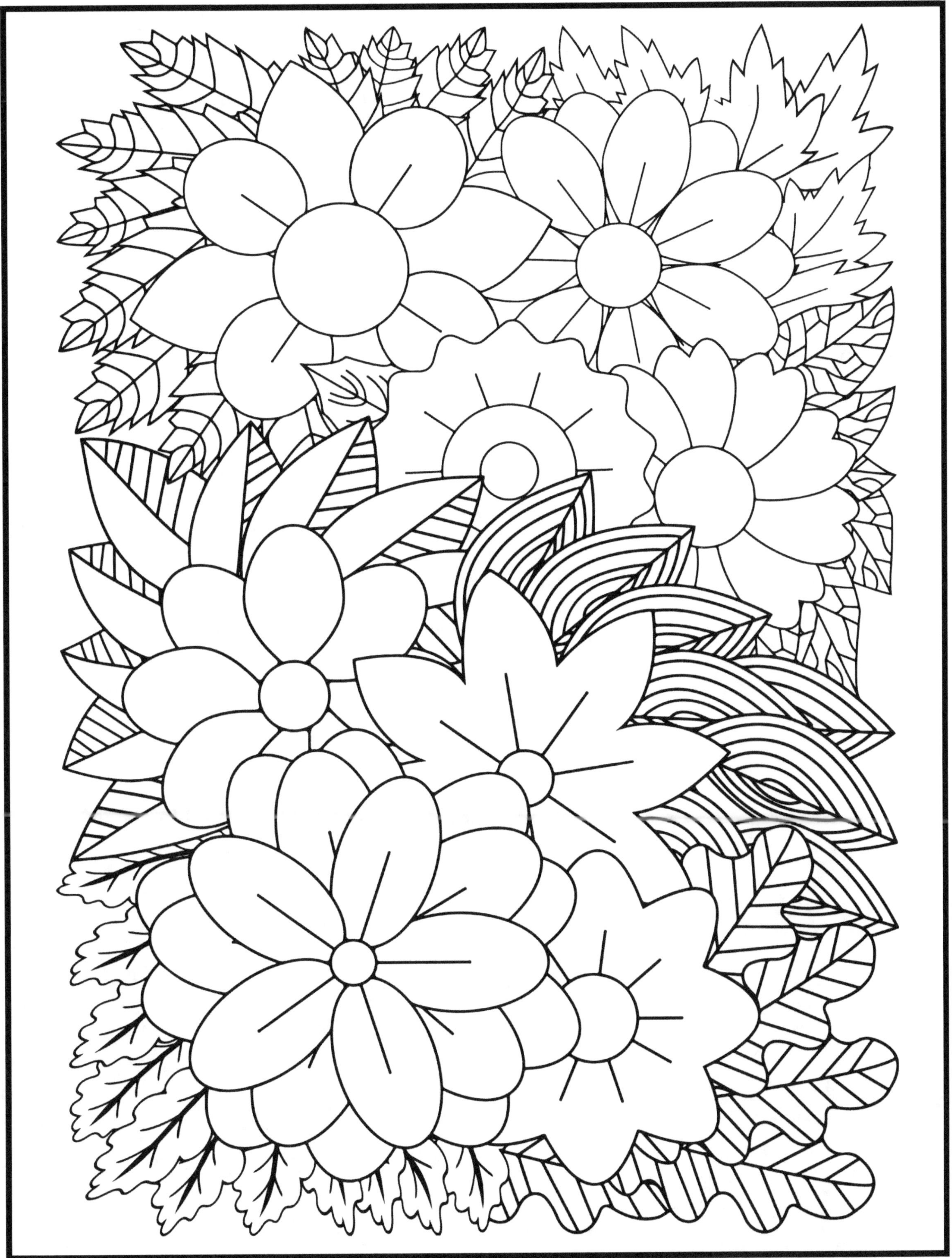

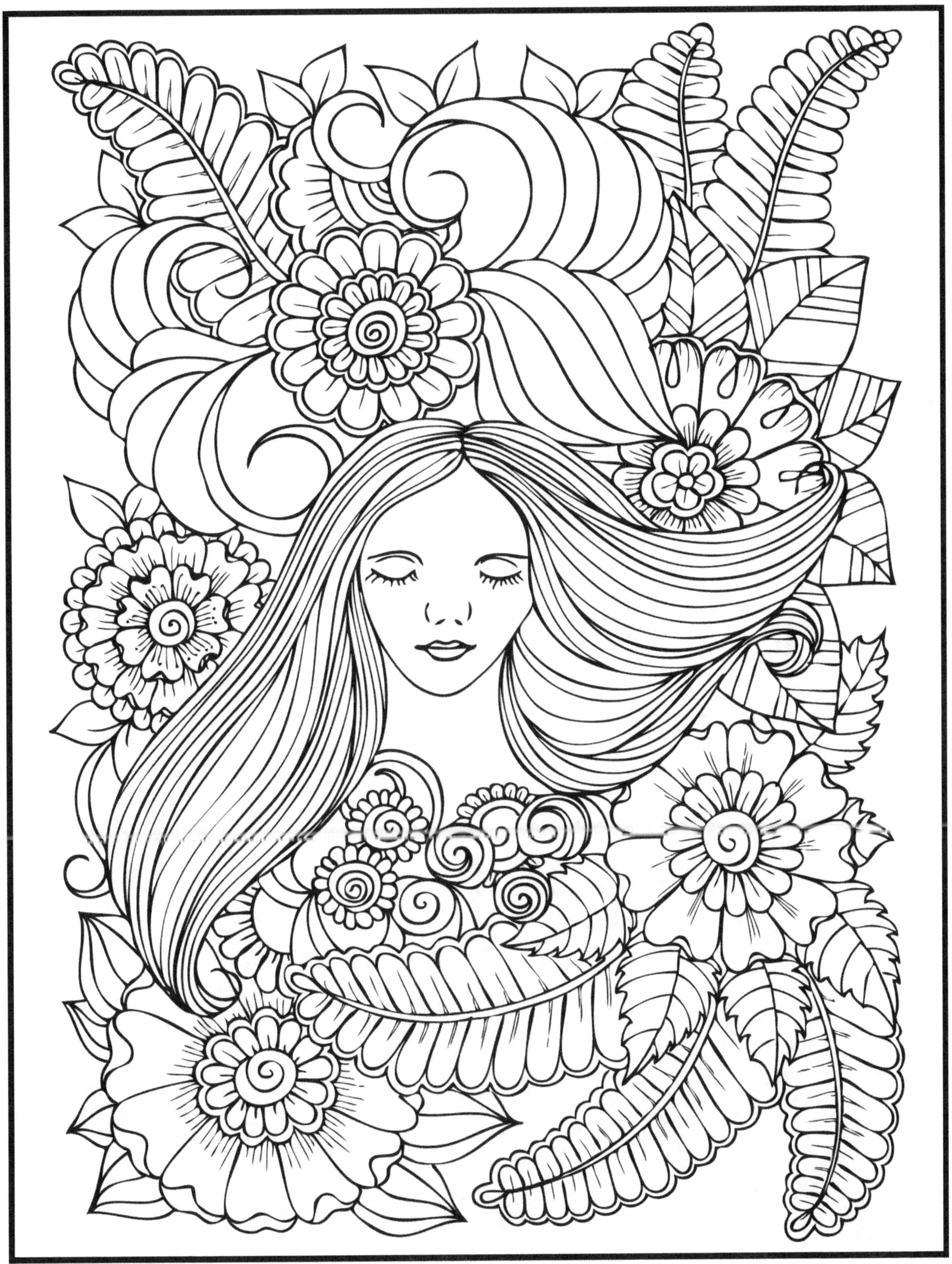

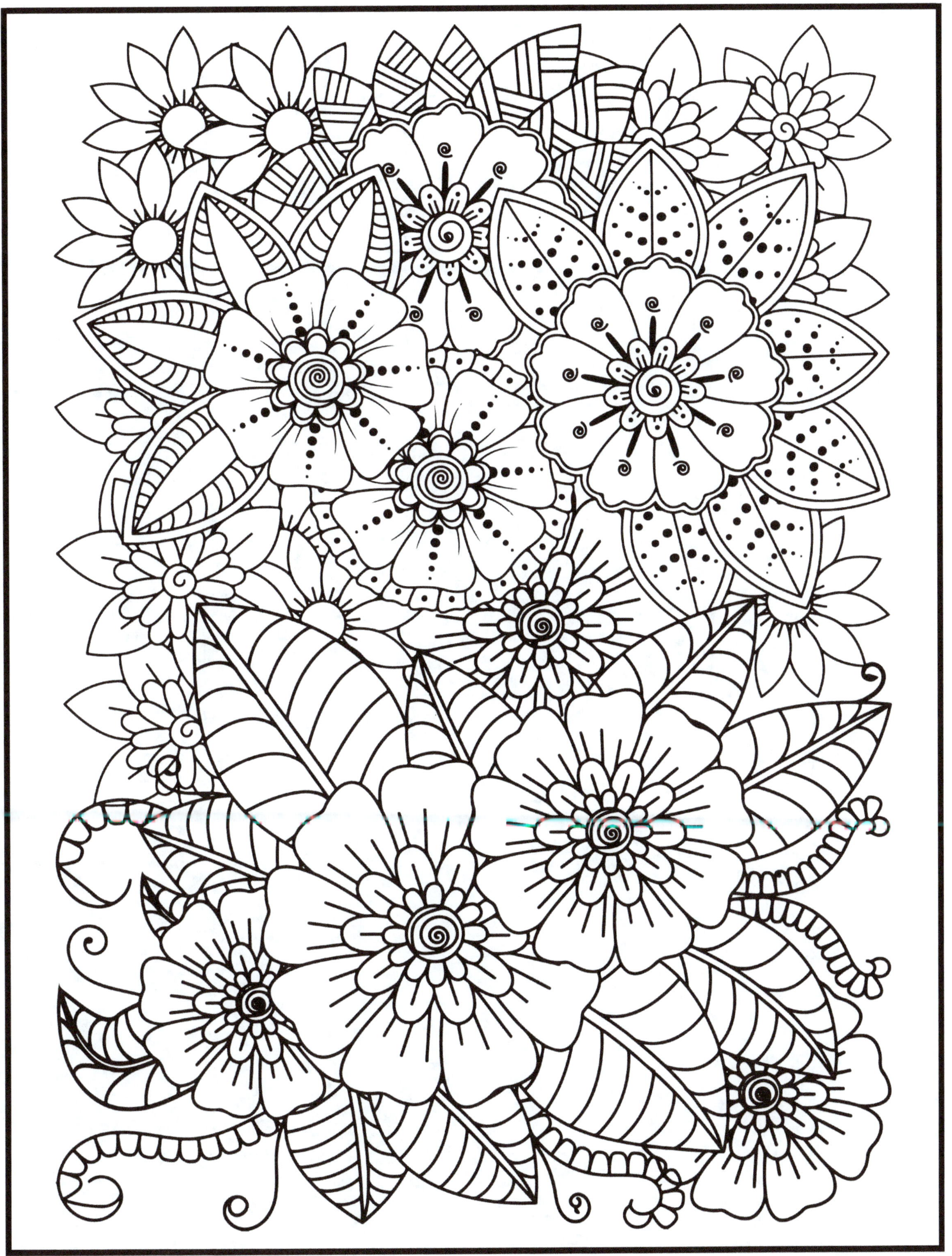

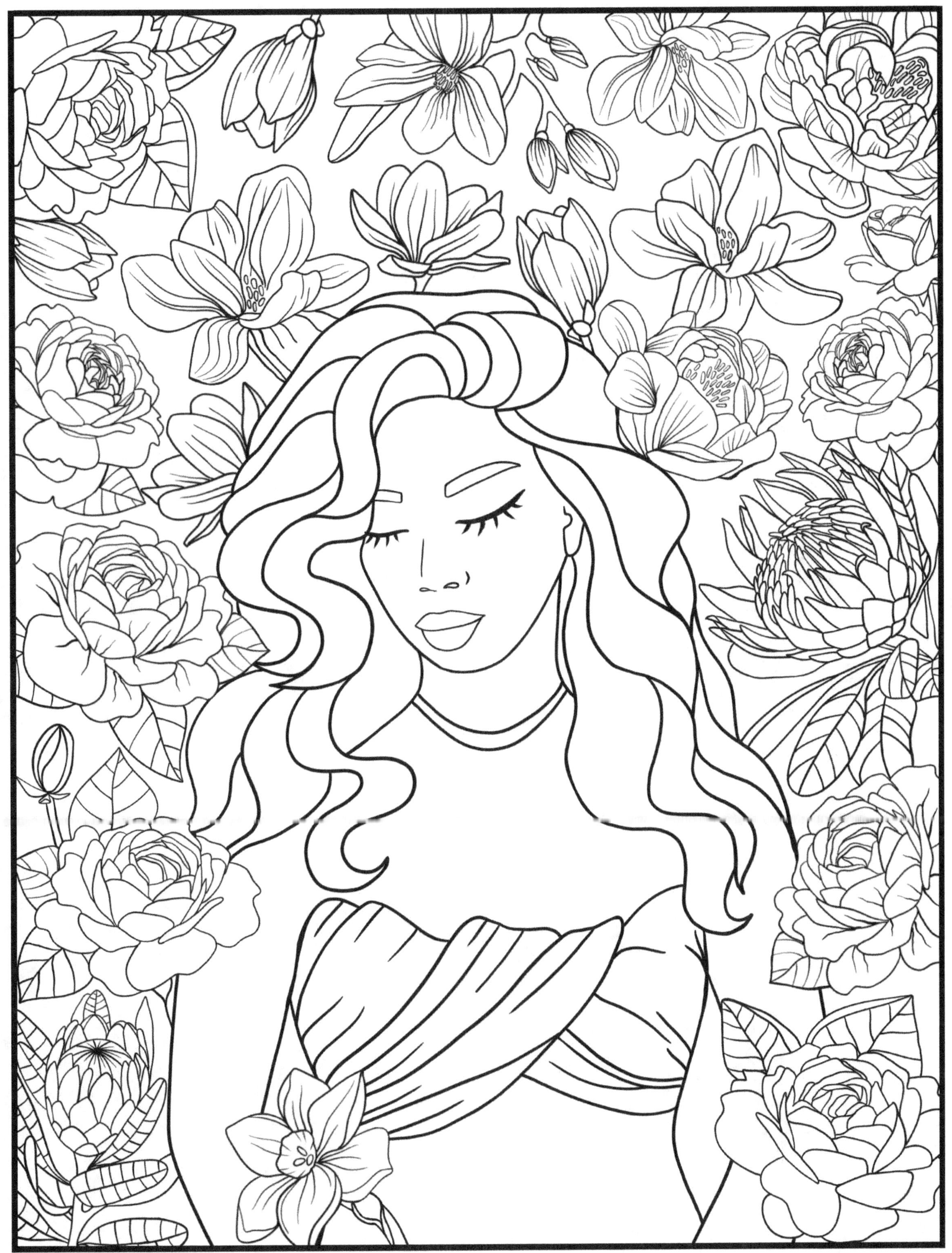

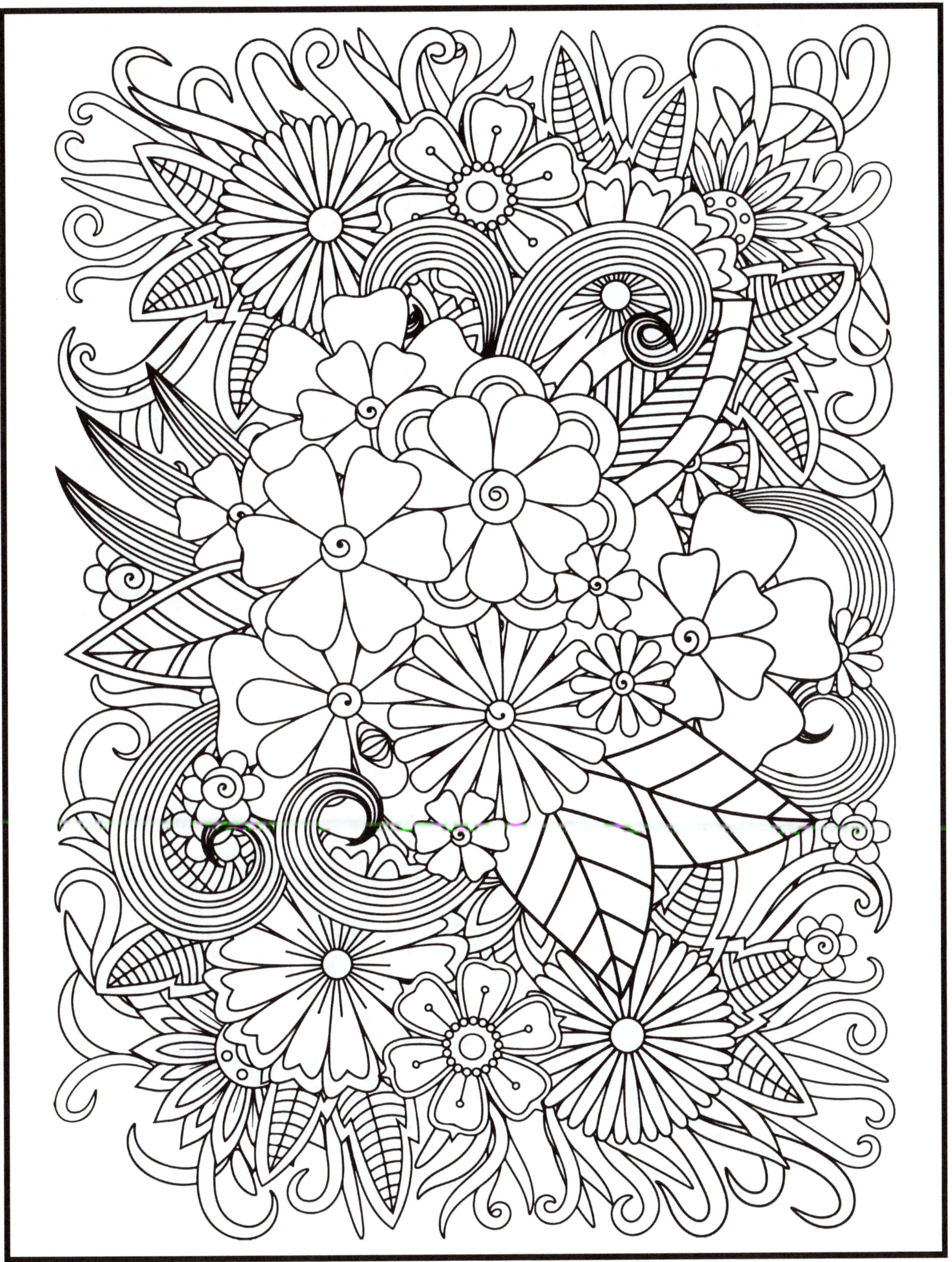

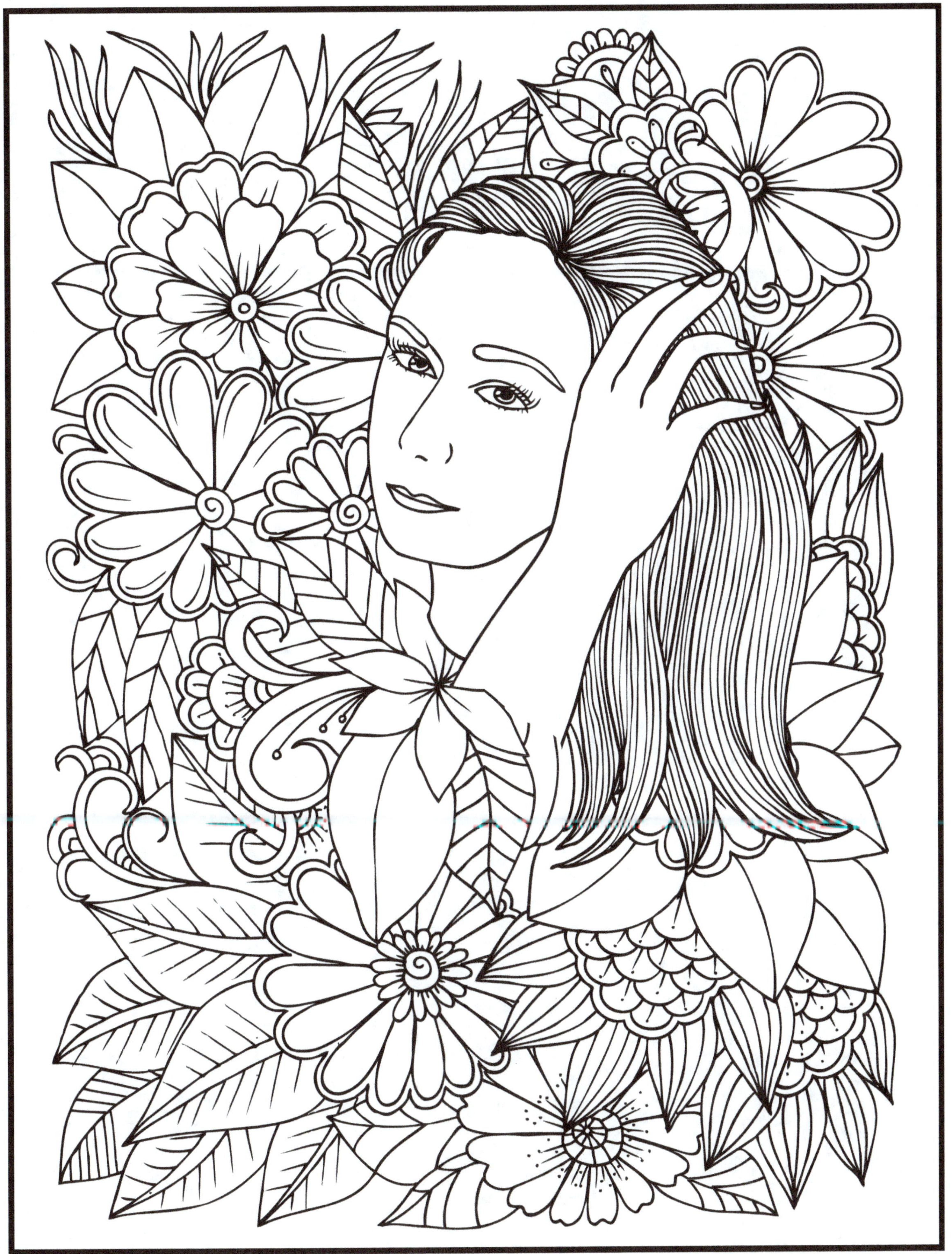

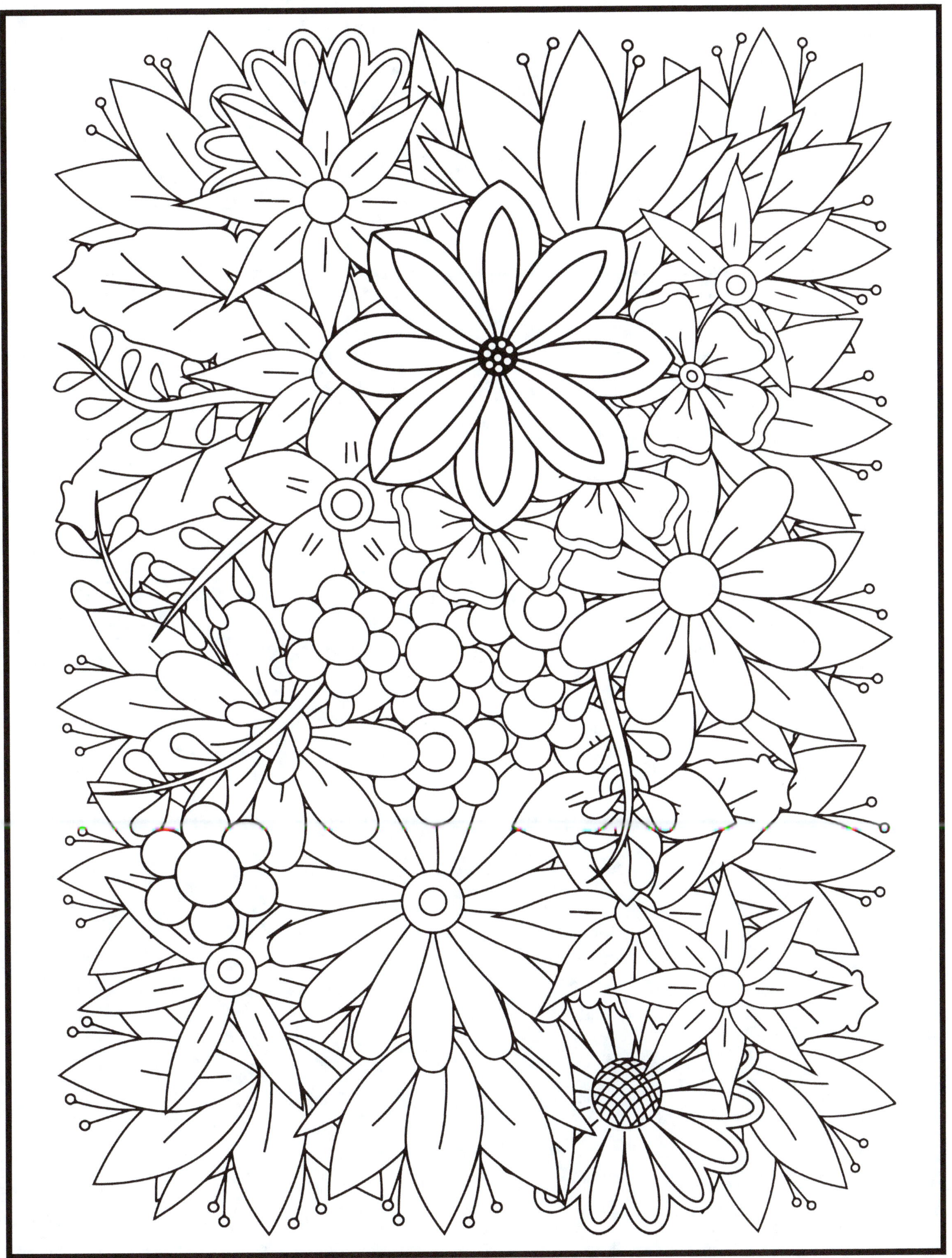

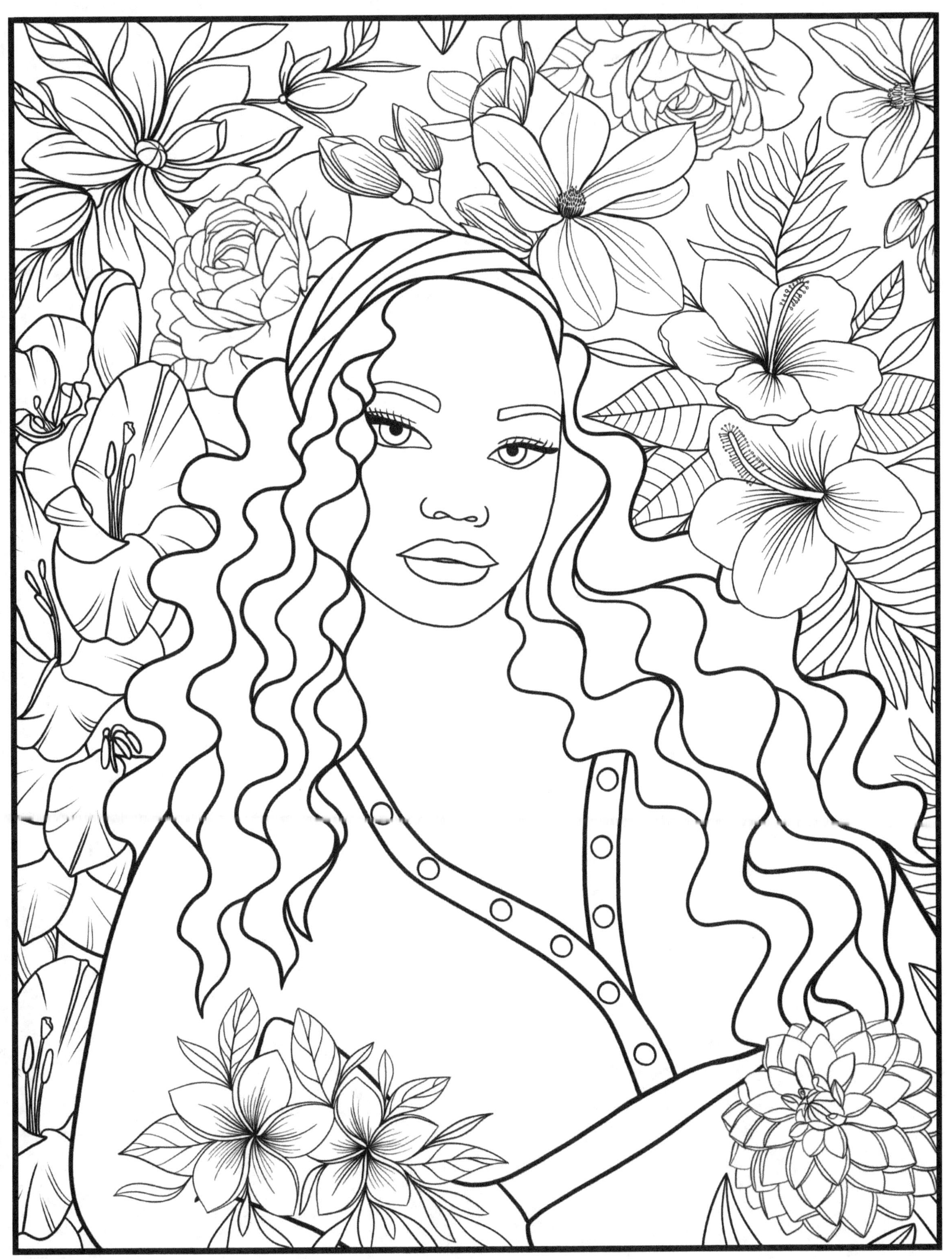

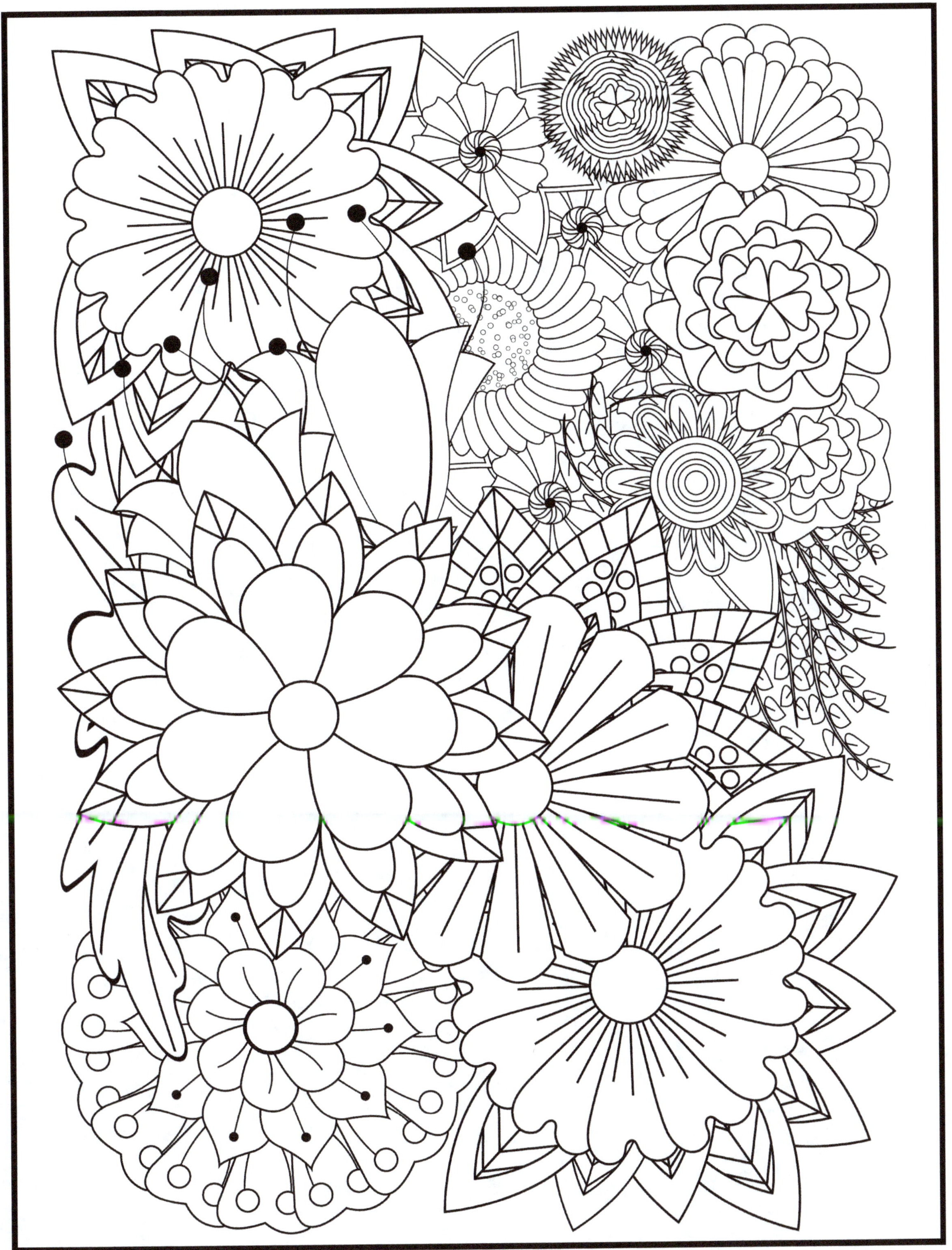

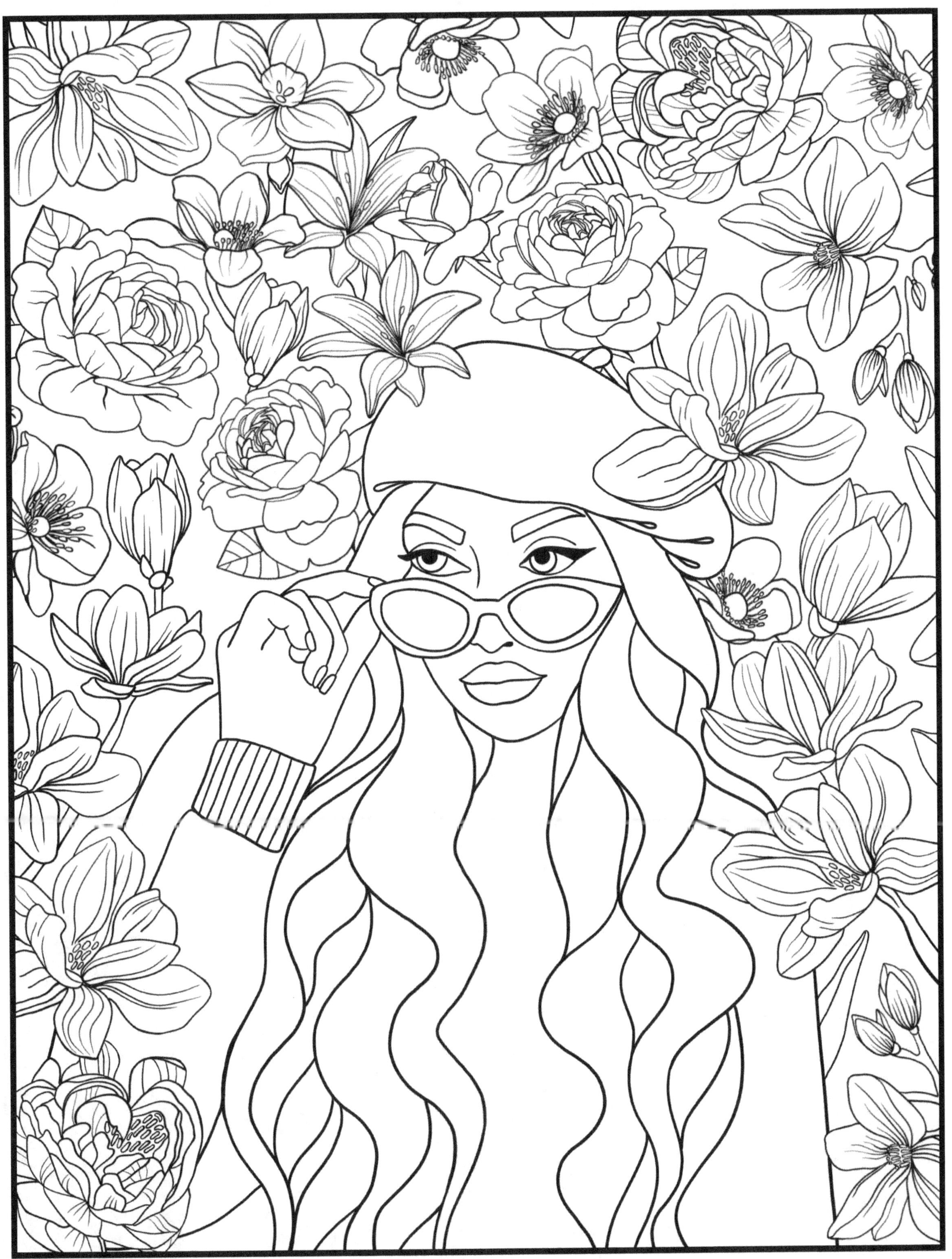

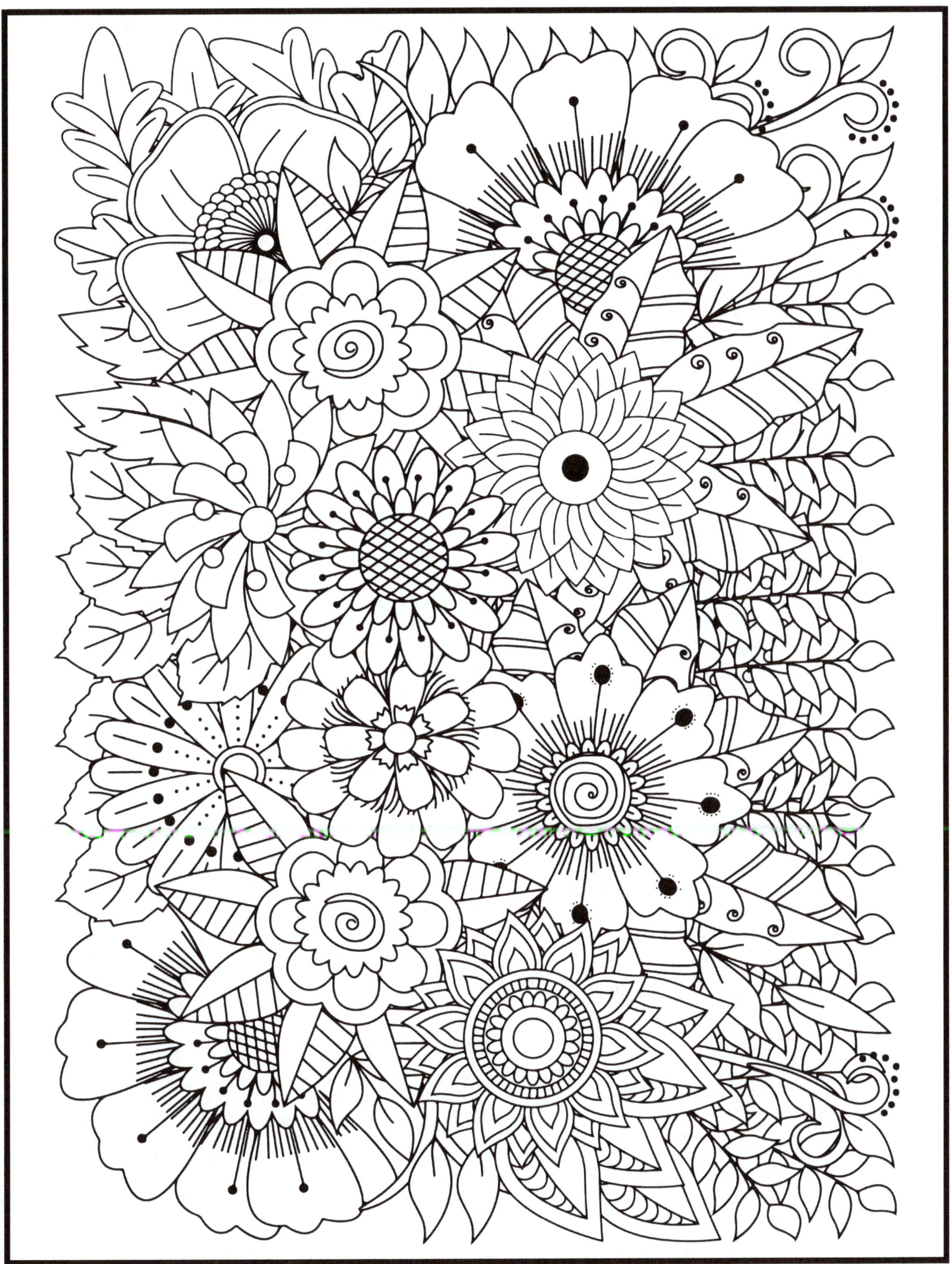

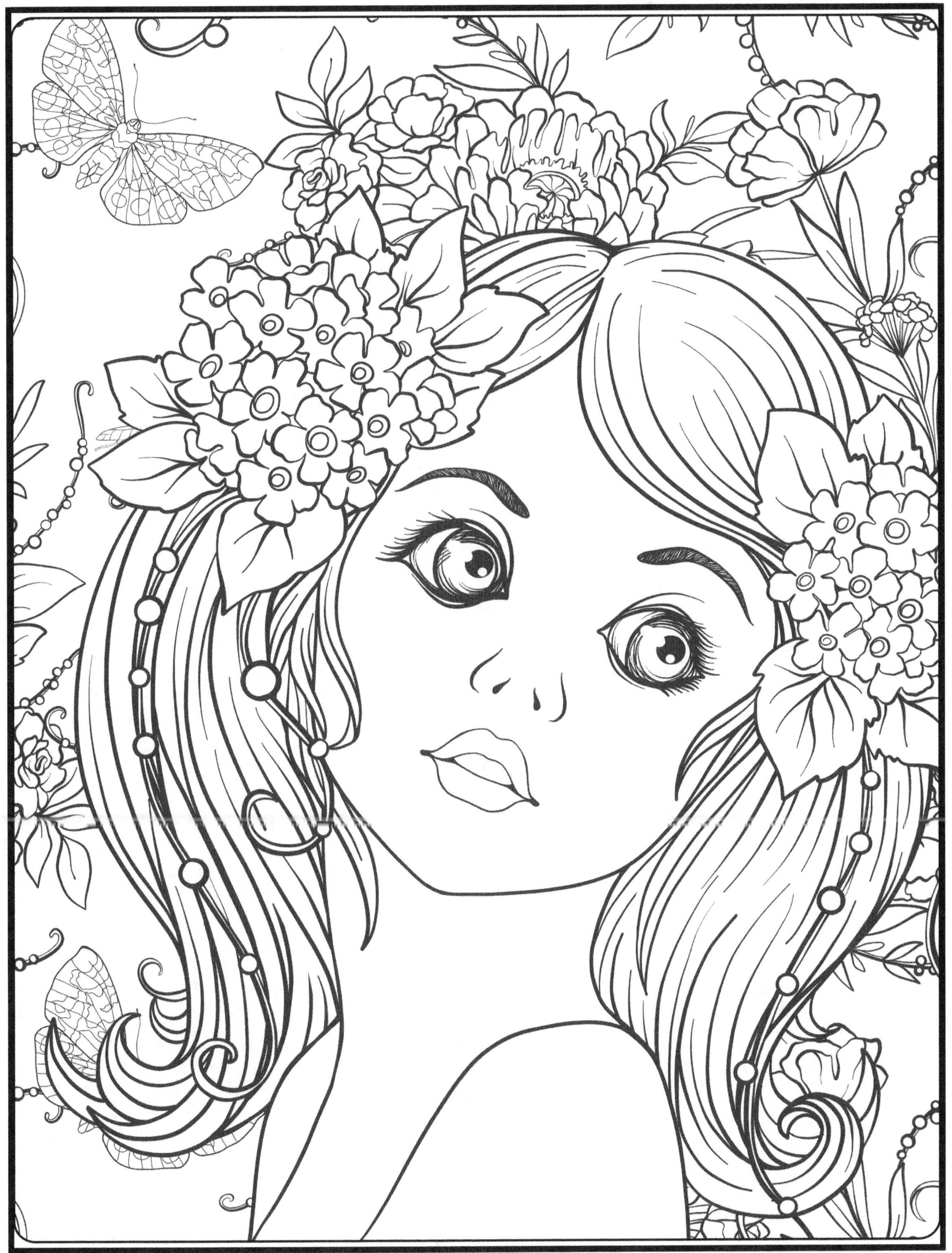

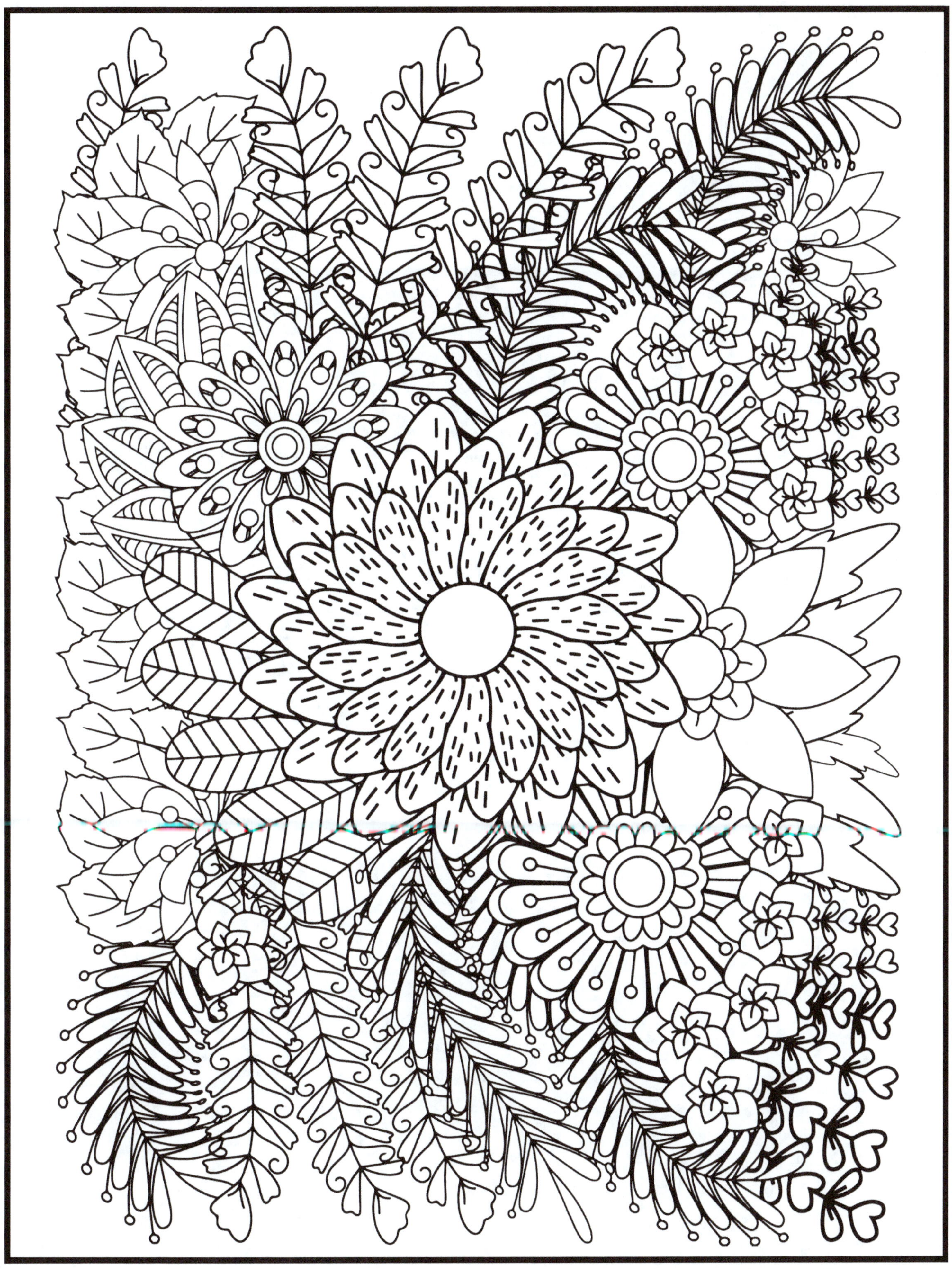

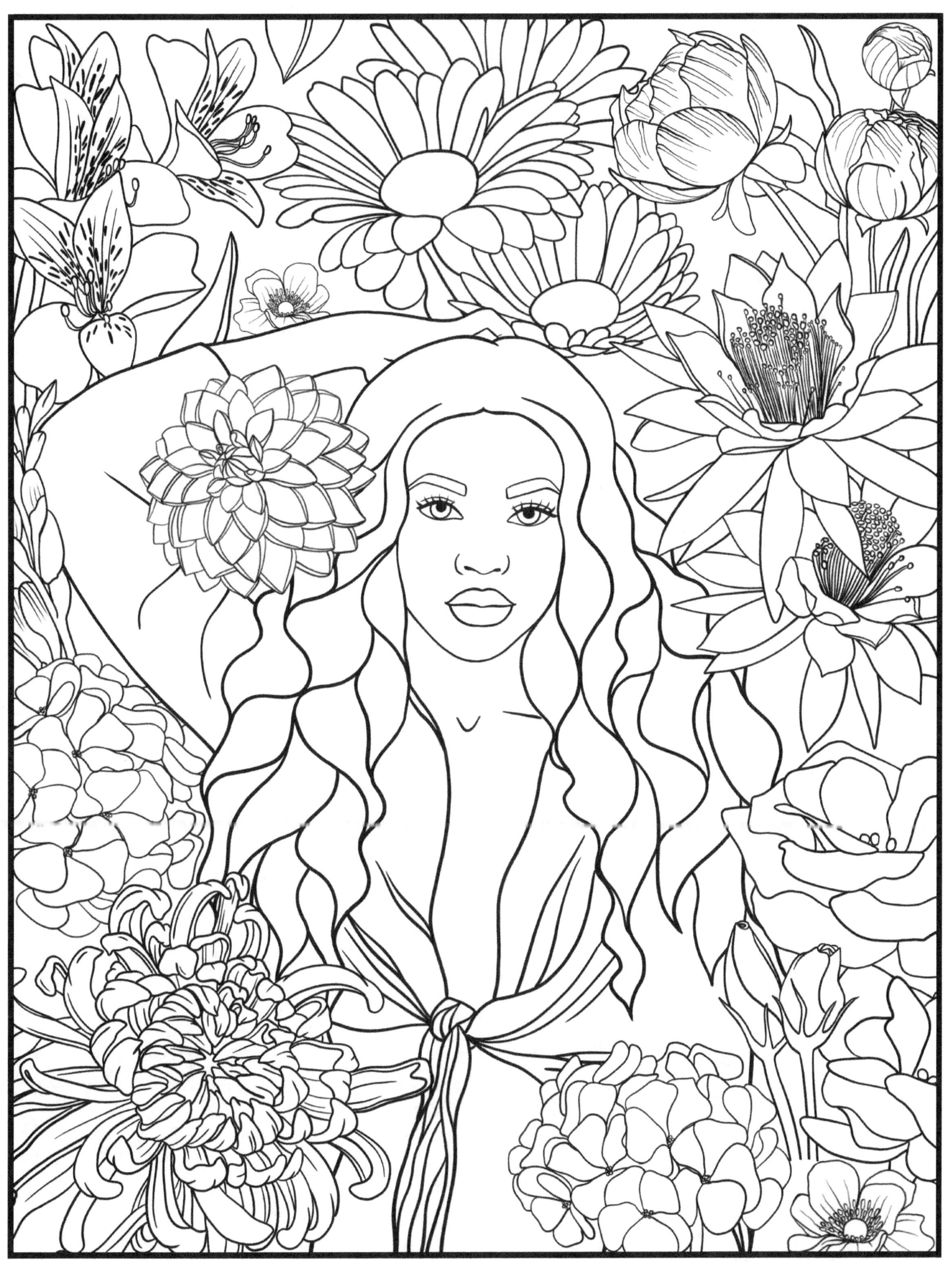

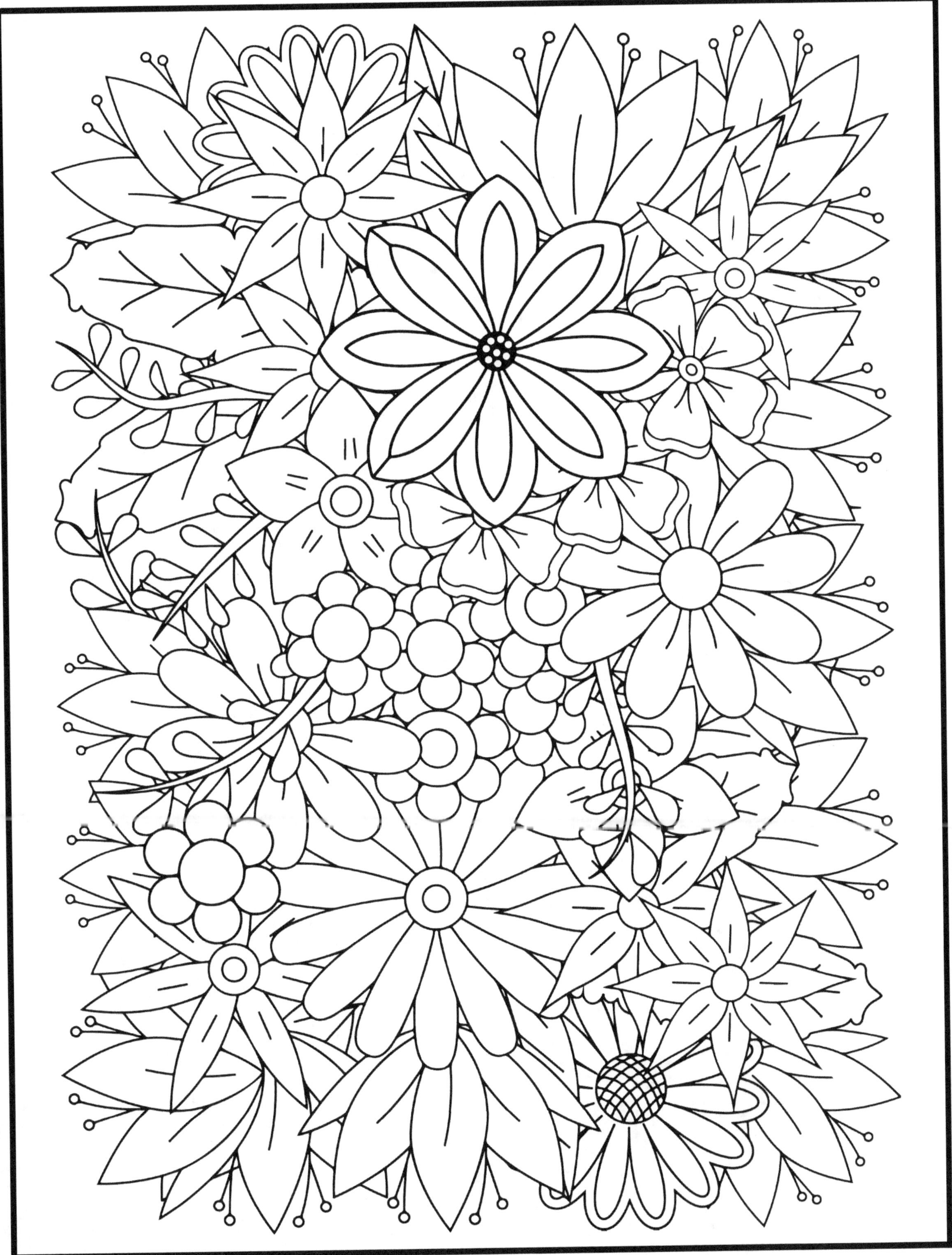

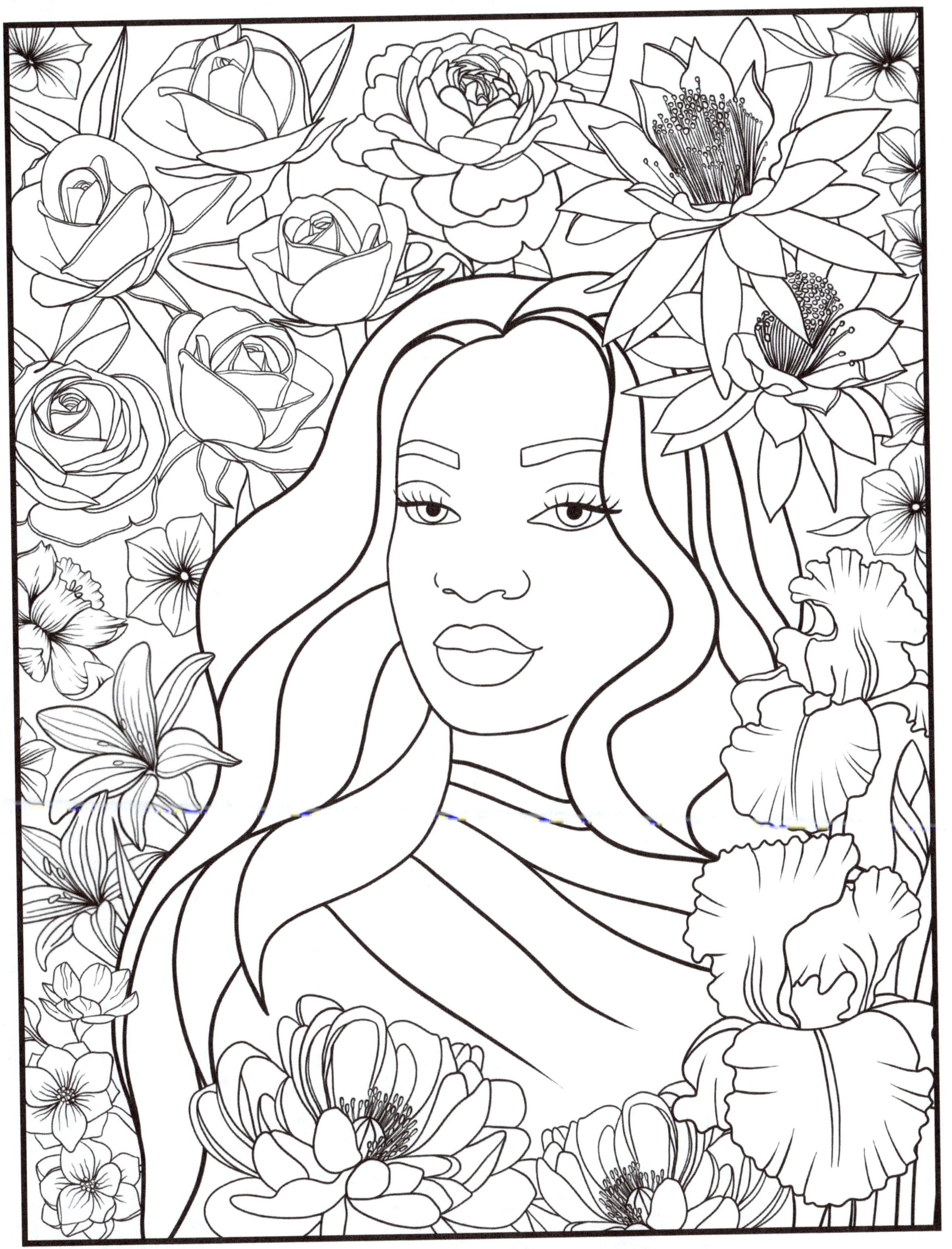

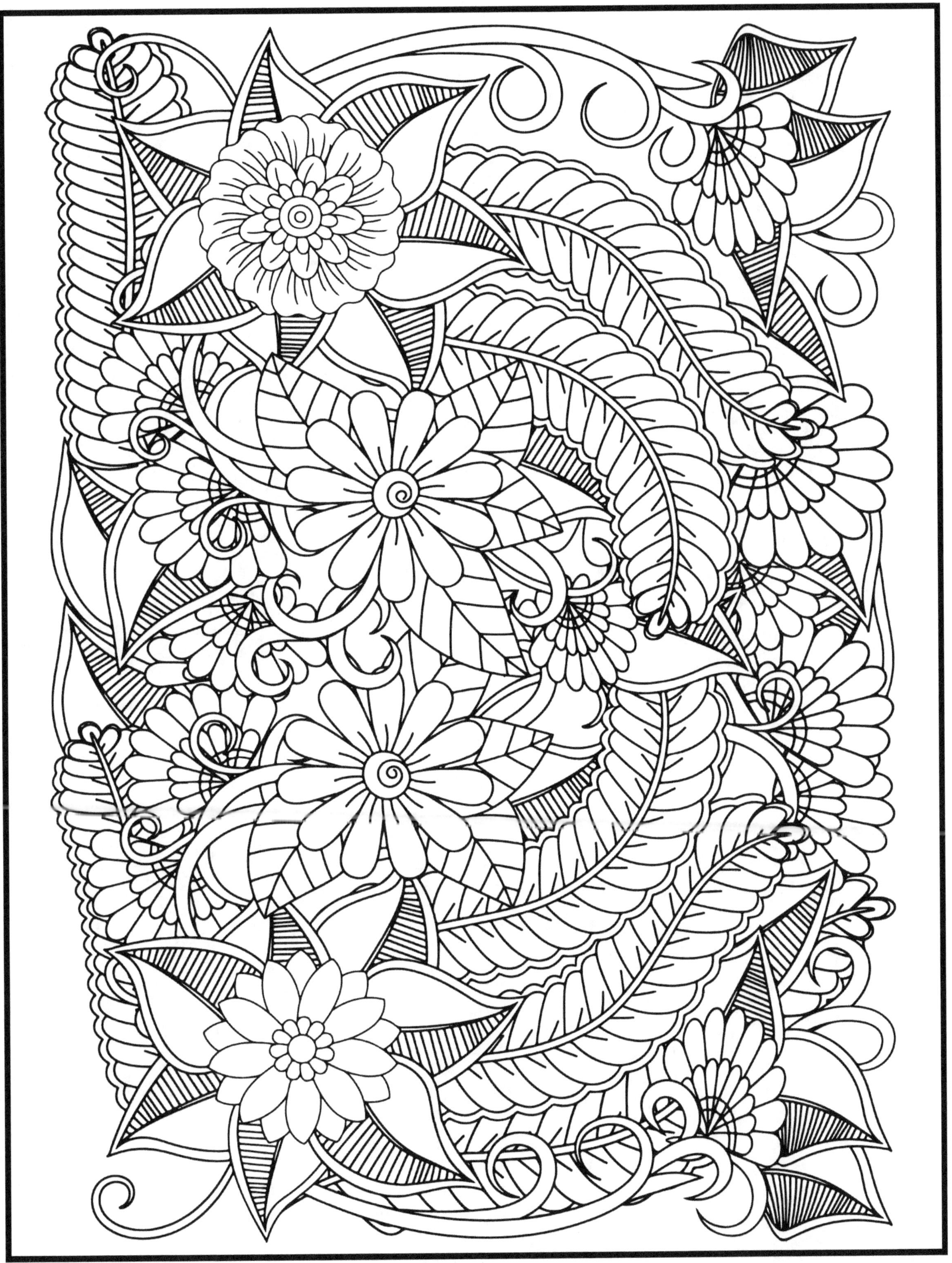

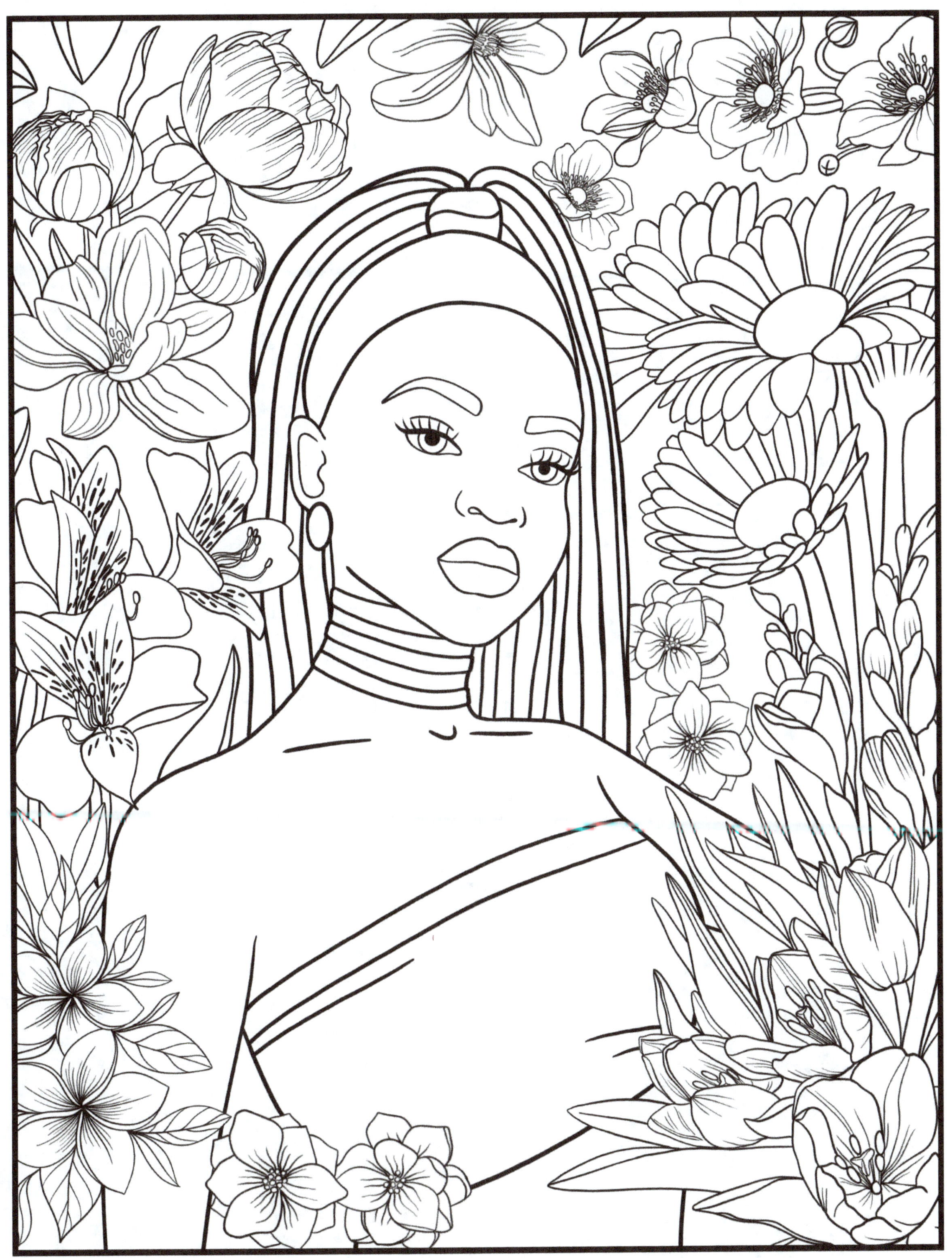

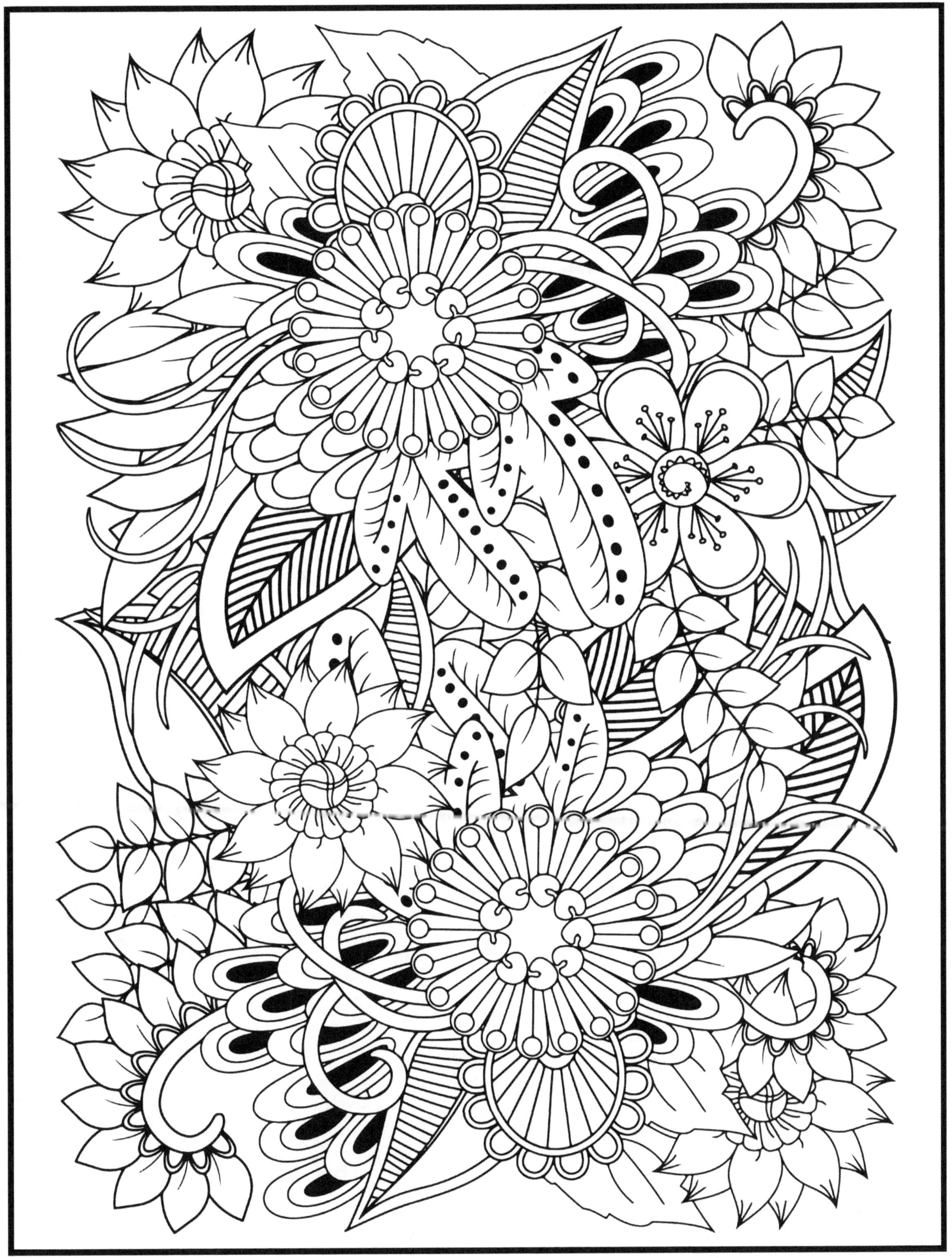

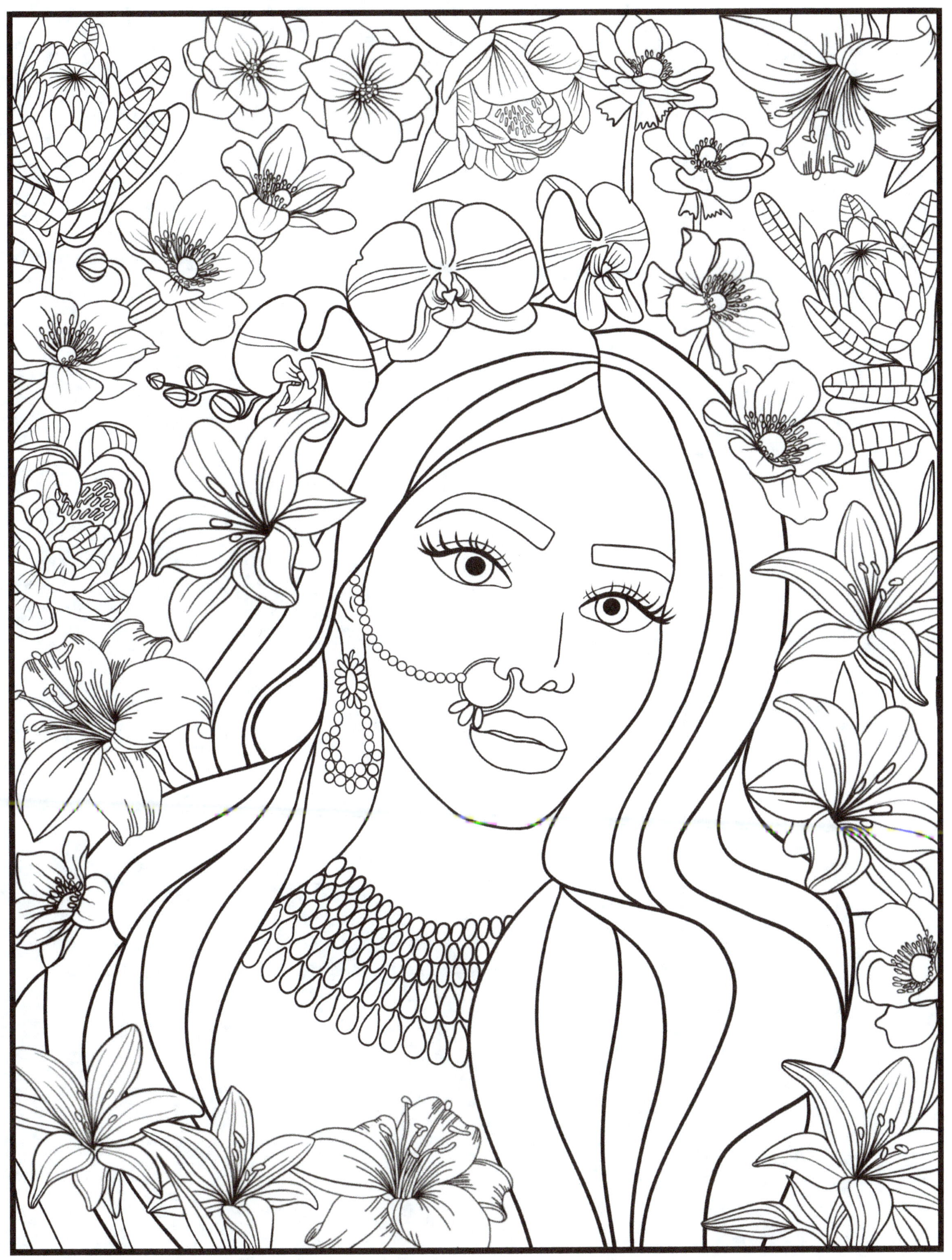

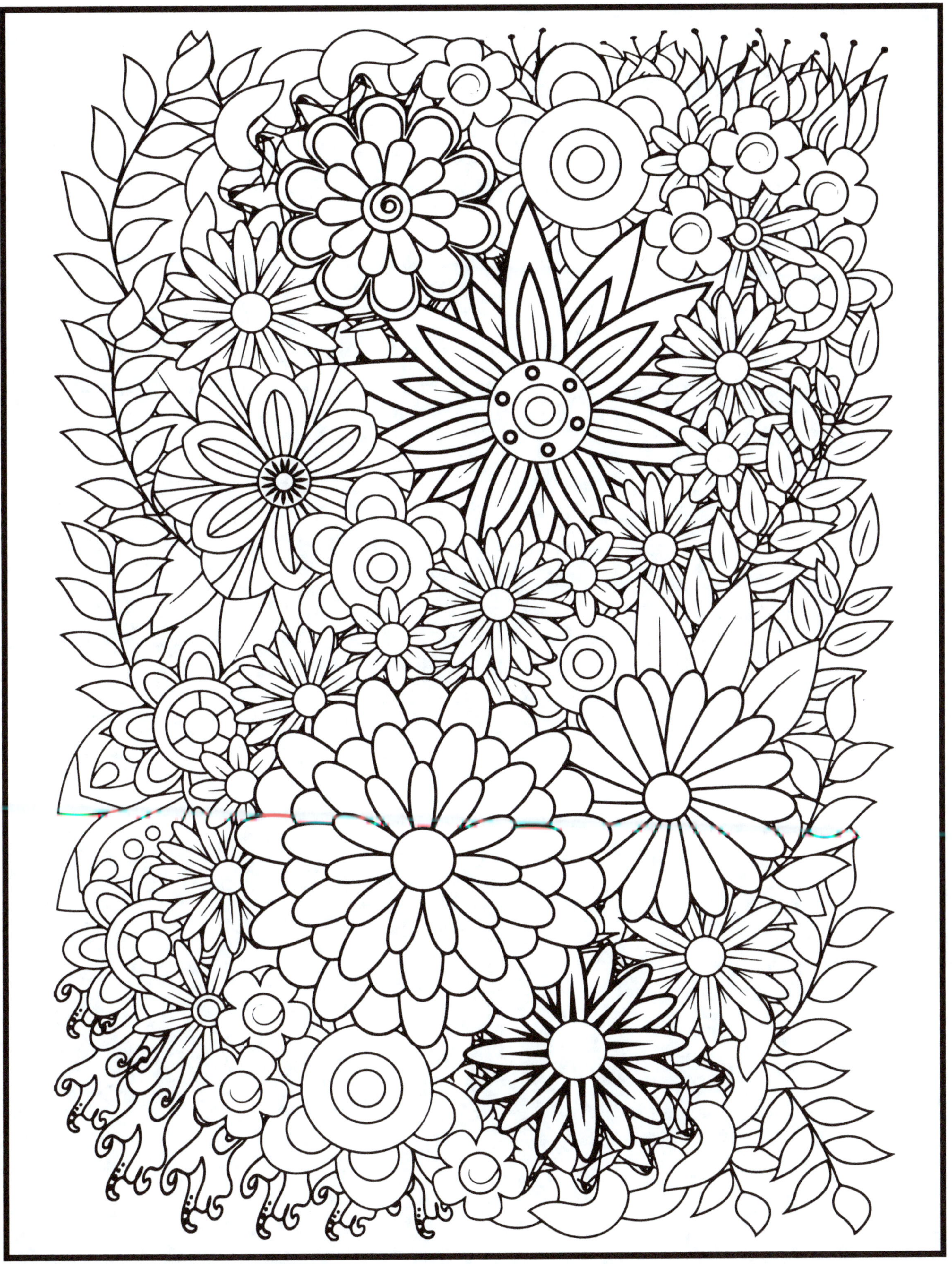

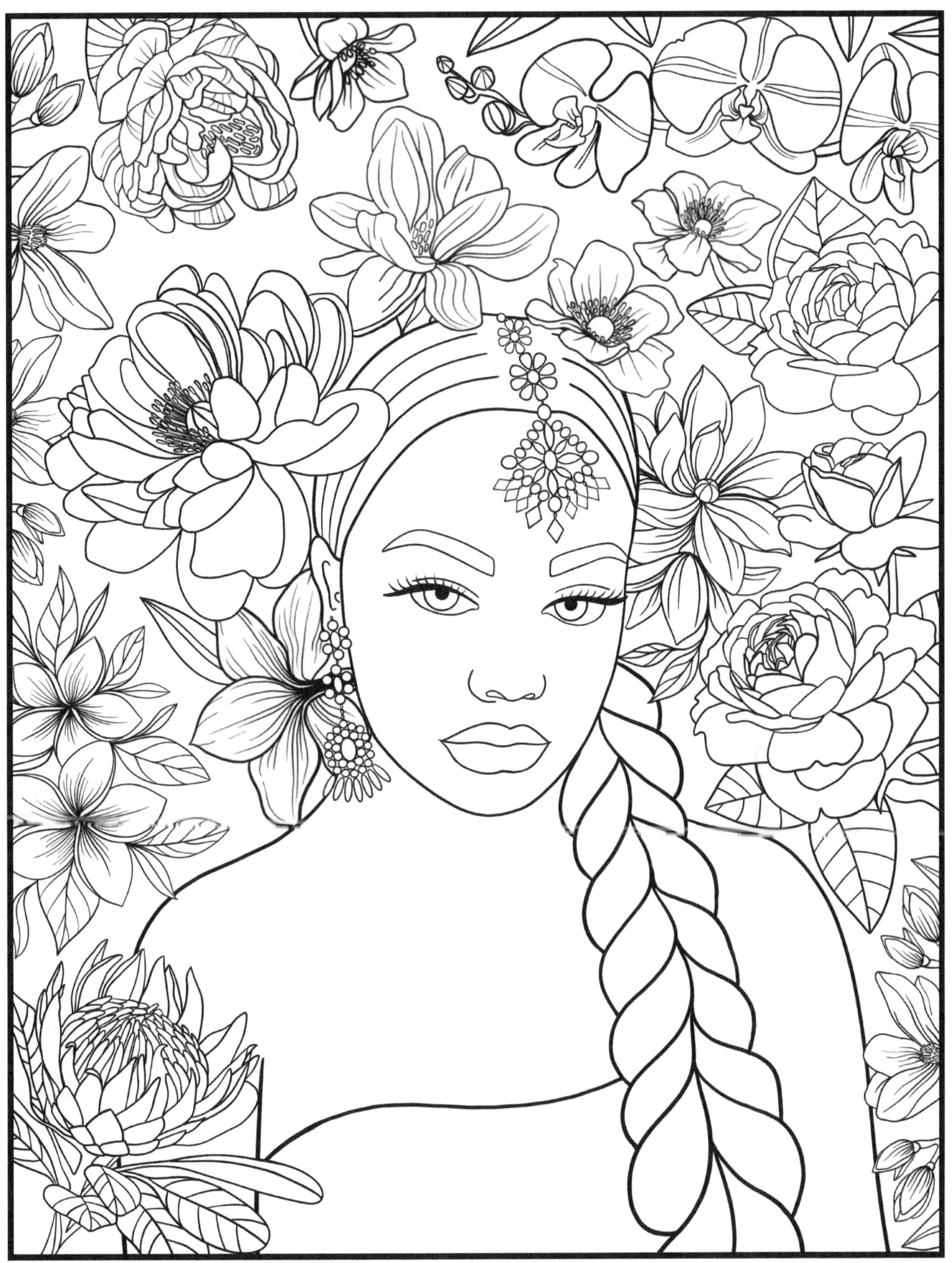

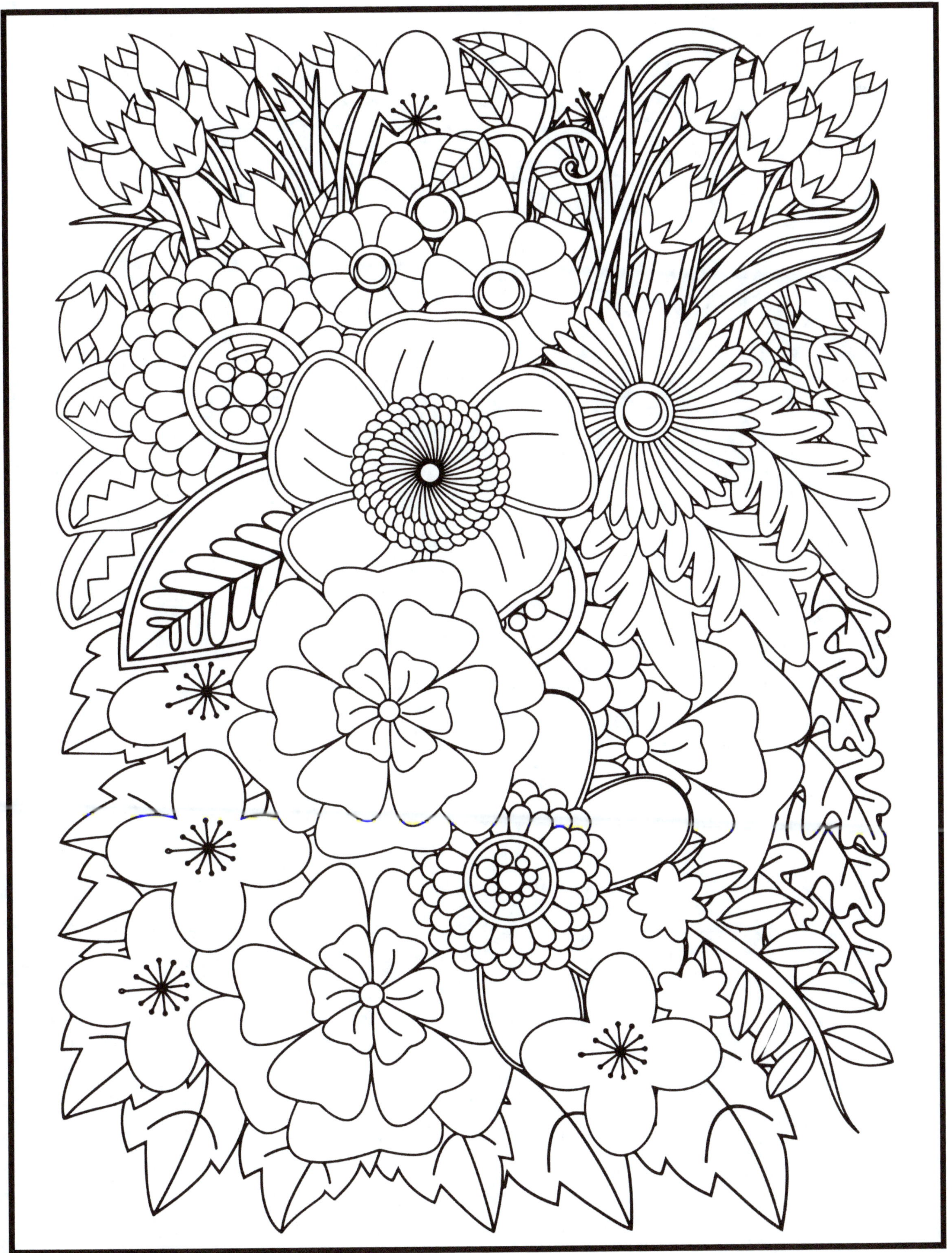

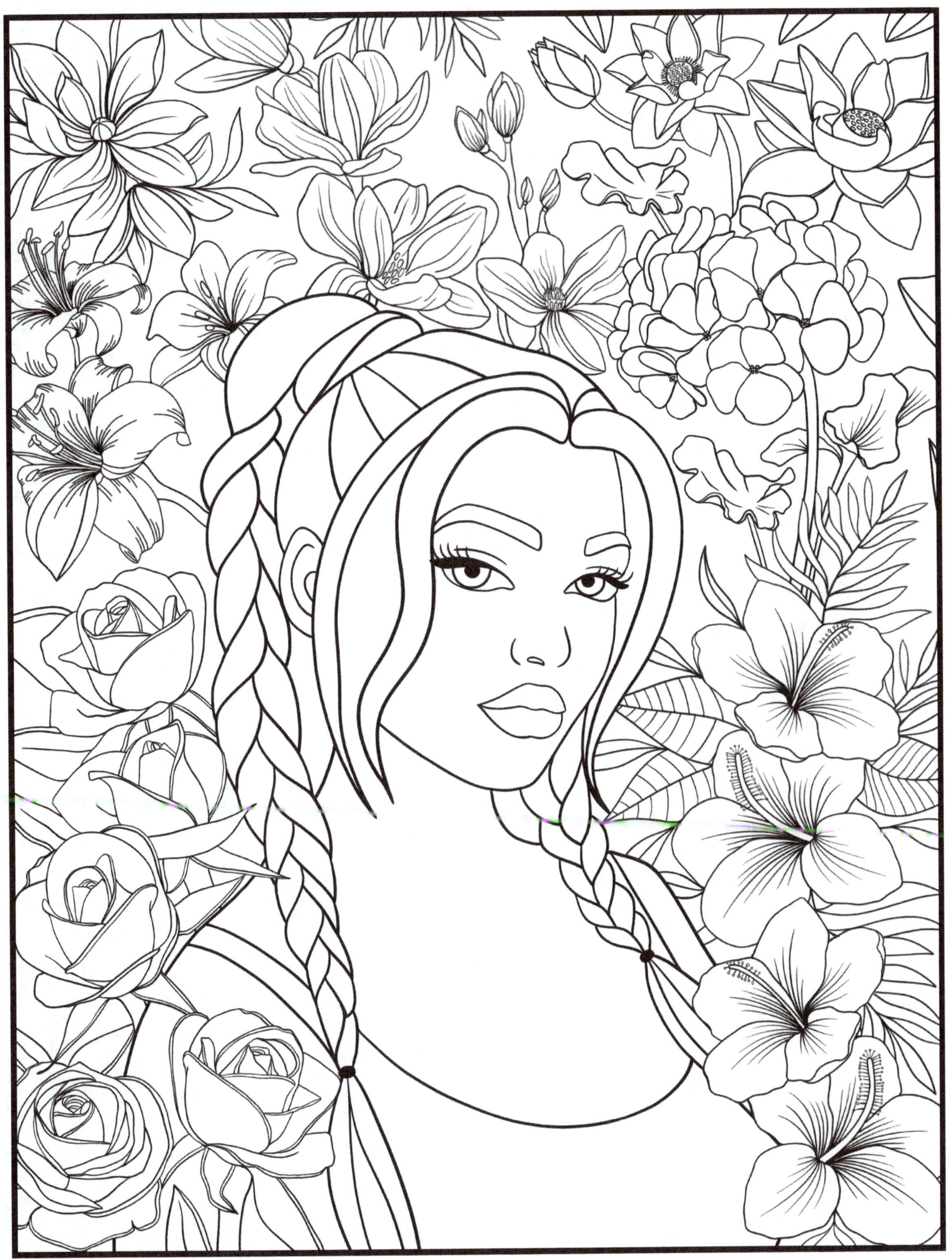

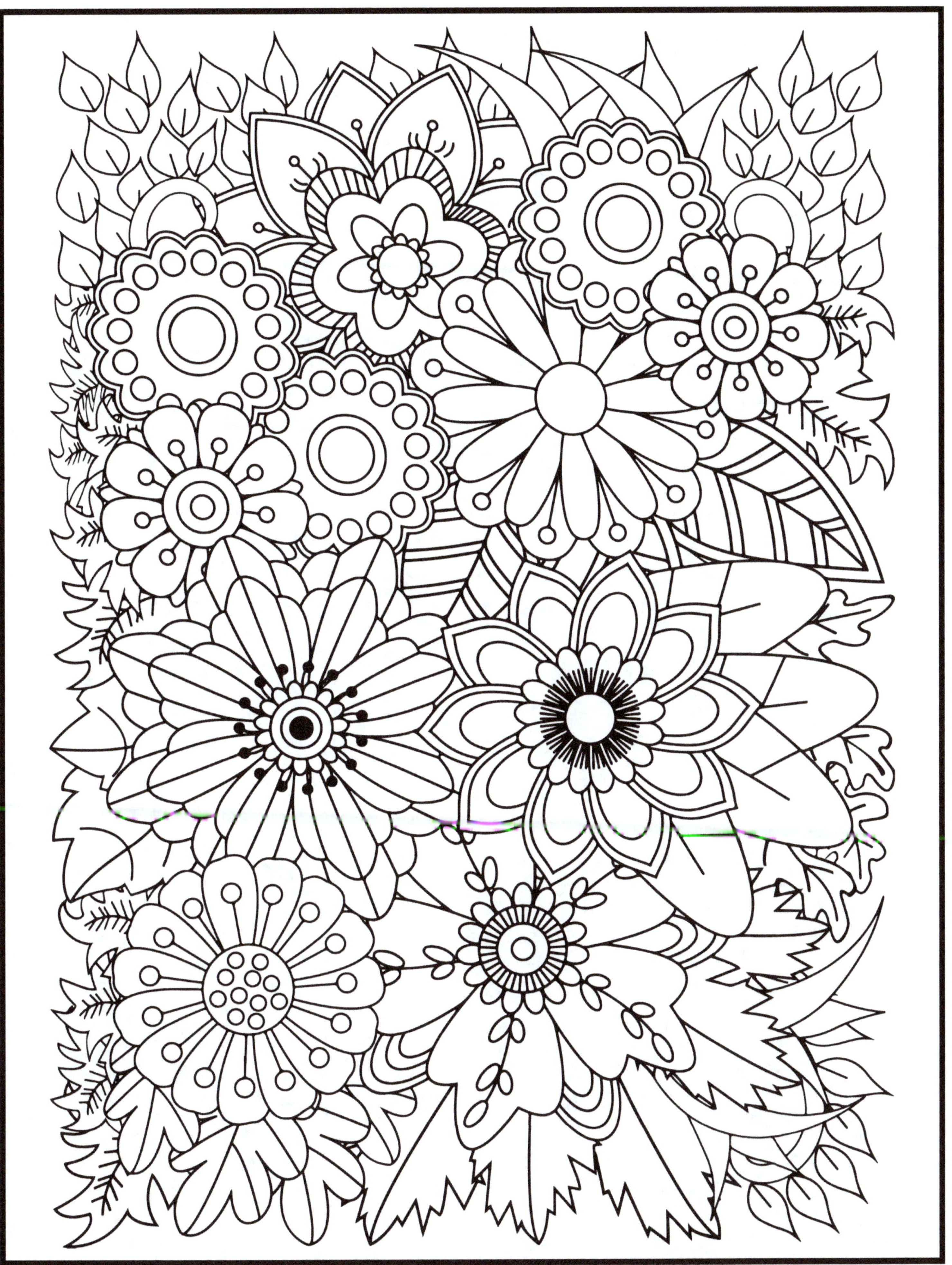

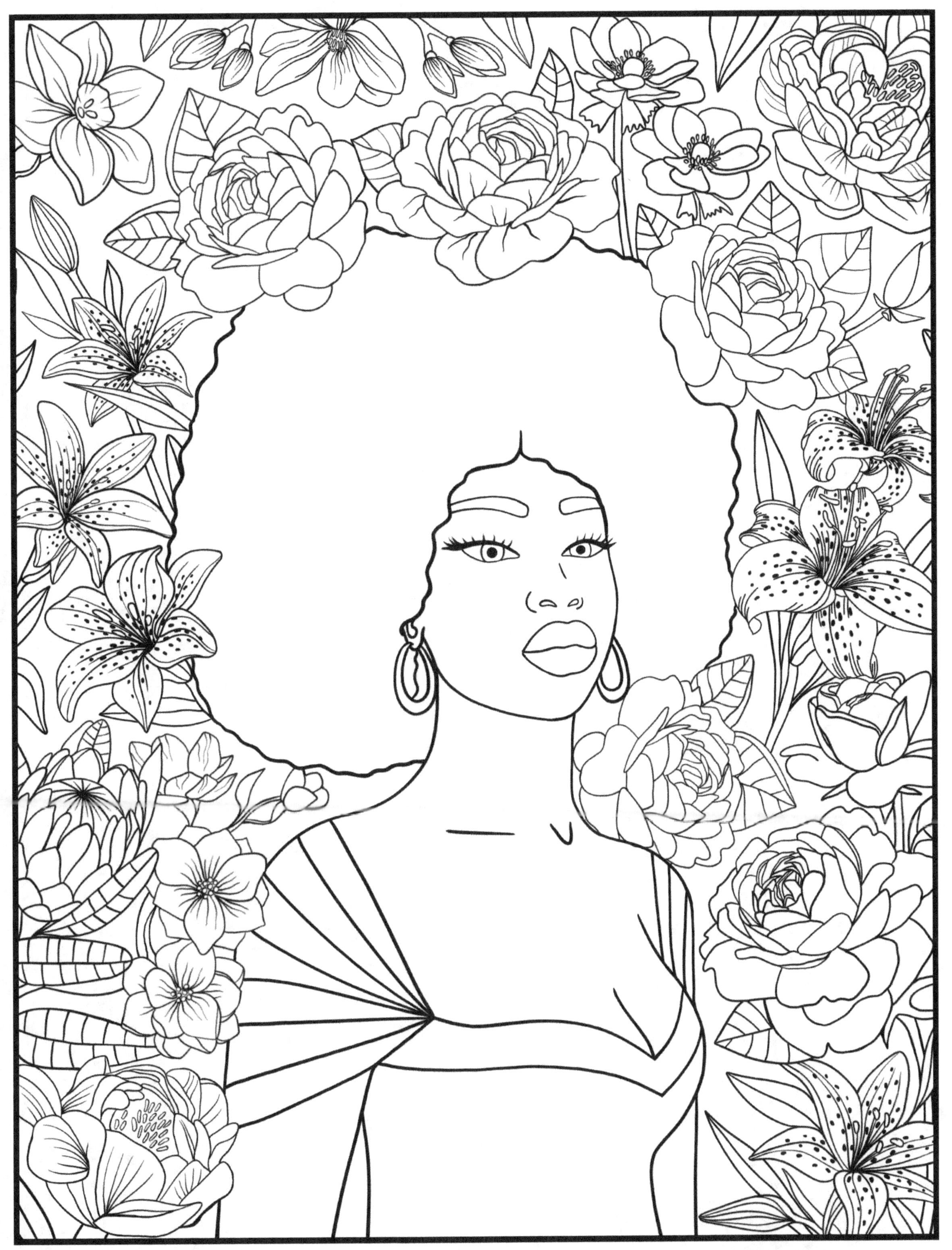

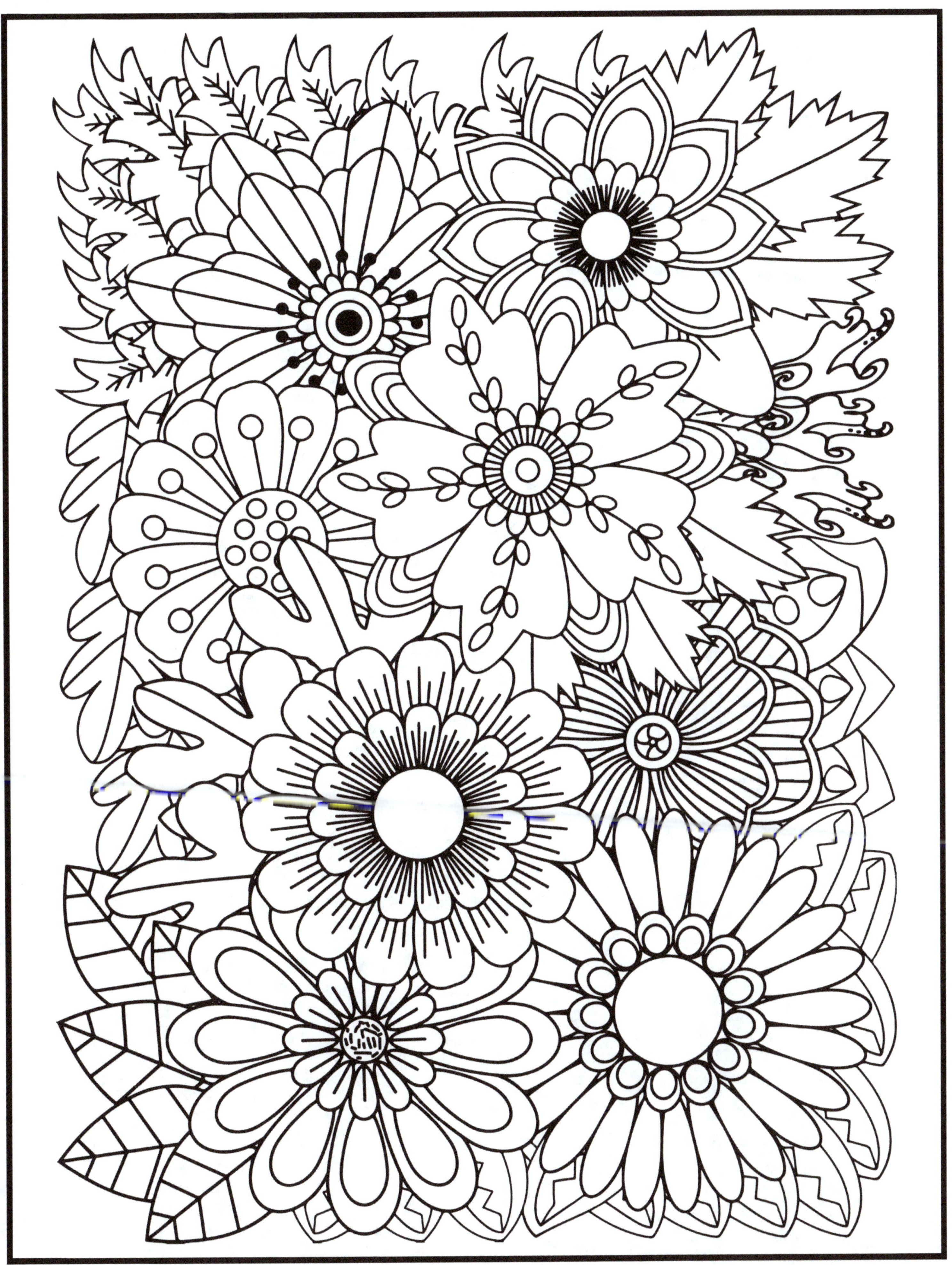

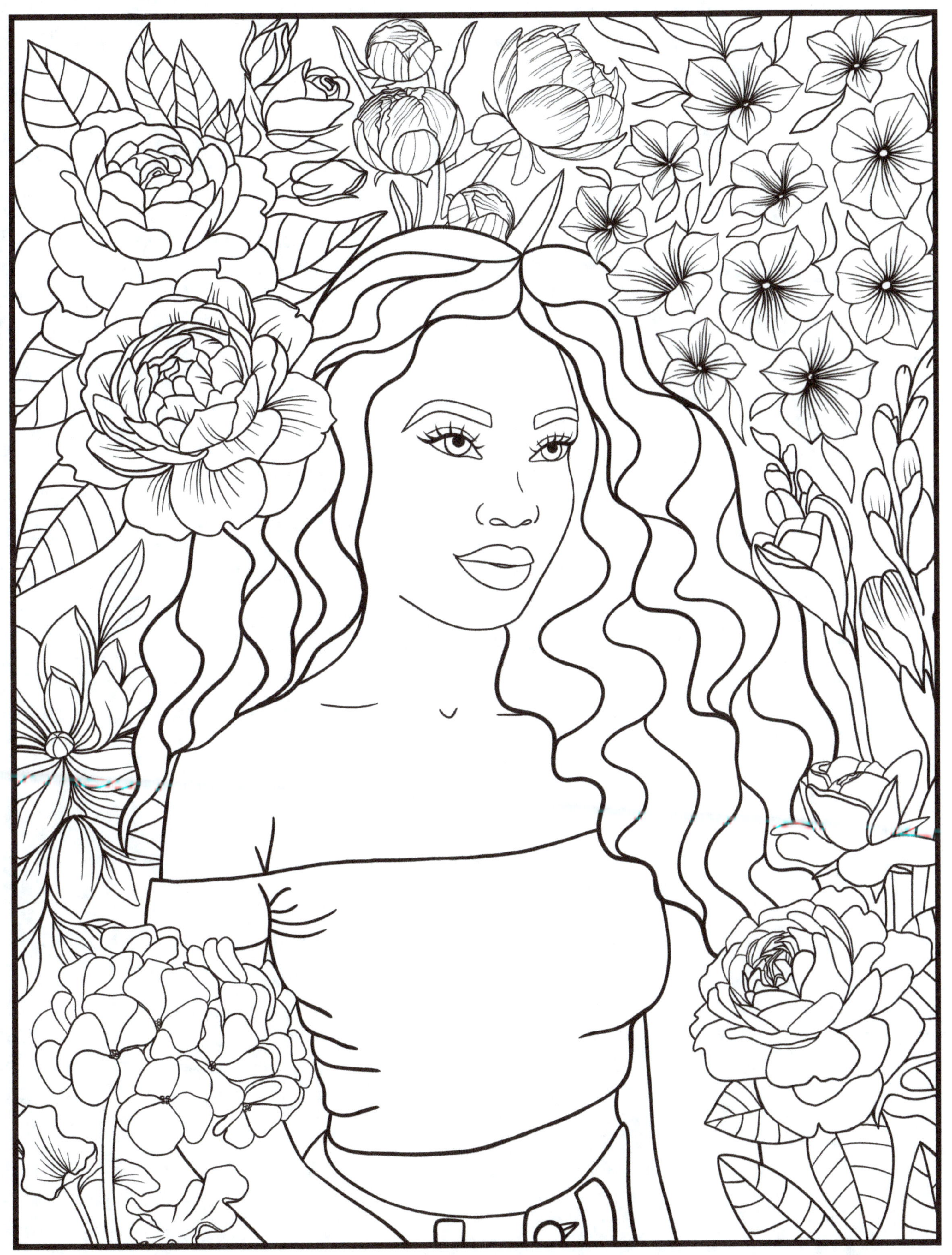

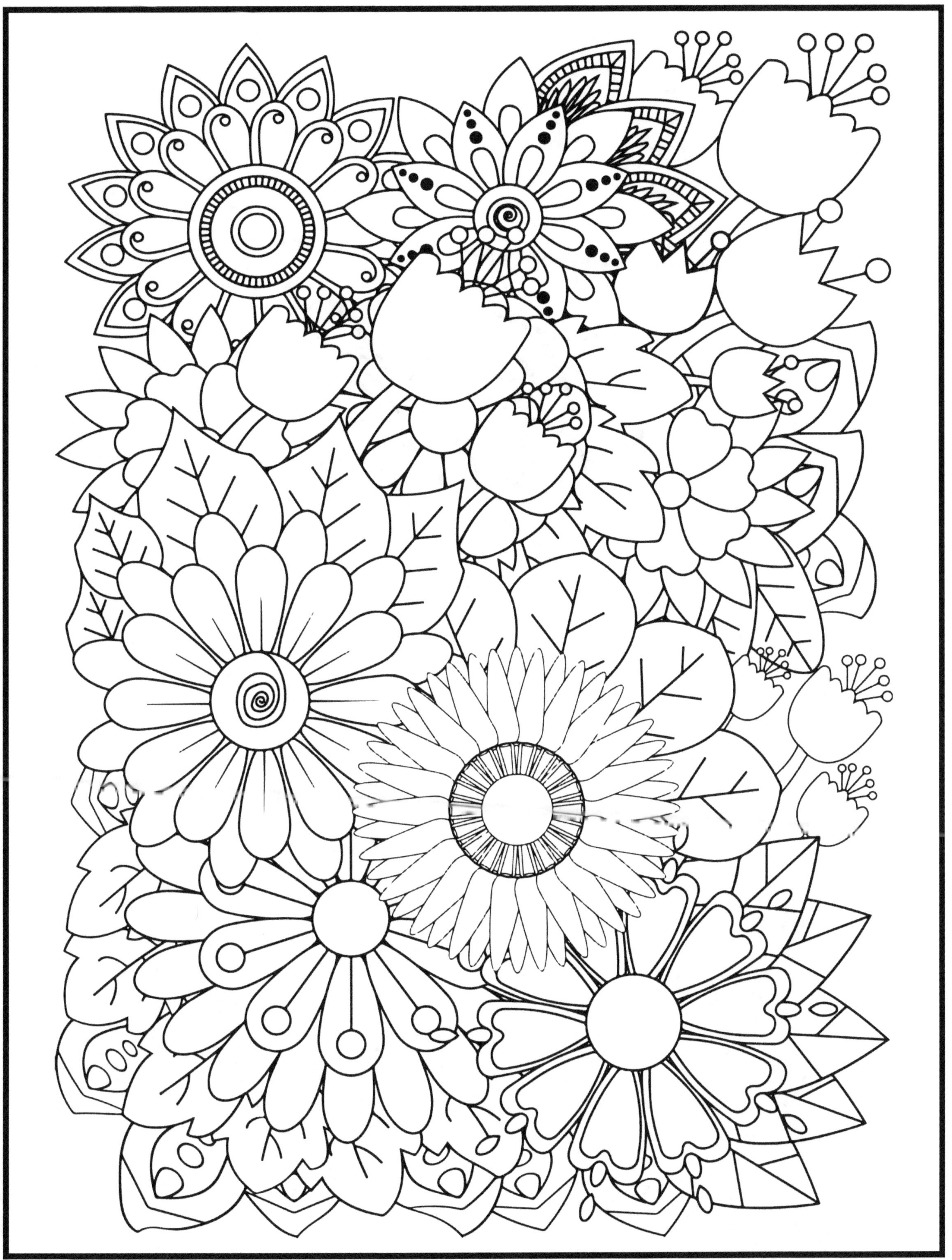

Thank you